Enjoy Getting the Dances You Want

Filling in the Blanks of Argentine Tango

–   Book One -

—

Table of Contents

Preface

There's a lot of heartache when it comes to getting dances. Because it doesn't matter if you're the best dancer on the planet if no-one will dance with you.

A lot of people believe that when you become a Good Social Dancer, you magically gain access to all the partners that you want.

Unfortunately, many experienced tango dancers can't clearly put into words what it means to be a Good Social Dancer, let alone how they achieve it. How do you find the tango venues that suit you best? What can you do to make yourself feel at ease in them? On the night when it all goes horribly wrong, how do you turn it around? And how do you get the partners you want?

There isn't even agreement on the correct way to invite someone, how it's supposed to work and whether some versions truly are a thing of evil? On top of that, there's also often a culture of fear. You are told in a thousand subtle and not-so-subtle ways that the other dancers are, at best, the competition, at worst the enemy. Hopefully by the end of this book, you'll see that's not the case.

But what about the other important things, like technique and musicality? Those and more will be addressed in the upcoming books of this series. For now, let's focus on getting the dances you want and having a good time at tango venues.

This isn't intended to be the Bible of the One True Way to dance tango. It's simply here to fill in the blanks for tango dancers of all persuasions and levels of experience. From how to enter the Milonga, to dealing with being manhandled on the dance floor, to Unicorn Glades. So get yourself a glass of something pleasant, sit back and let's talk about social tango.

Oliver Kent, Winter 2016

A brief note on pronunciation

Tango involves a lot of words that may be new to you and aren't obvious how you should pronounce them.

In Spanish there is one clearly defined stress per word. For example, "Argentine Tango" has the emphasis on "AR-jen-teen TANG-oh". Also, "I" is pronounced "ee". So "milonga" (*the place where tango dancers go to dance socially, as well as a rhythmic style of tango music*) isn't "mil-onga", it's *"mee-LON-ga"*. "Buenos Aires", (*the capital of Argentina and the spiritual home of Argentine Tango, often abbreviated to BsAs*) is pronounced "BWEN-oss EYE-reez". "Di Sarli" (*a famous Argentine tango composer, pianist and orchestra leader*), becomes "Dee SAR-lee", rather than "Dis-arli" and so on. "Villa Urquiza" (*a specific style of tango dancing, as well as an area in Argentina*) is pronounced *"VEE-zha ur-QUEE-sah"*

However, among native English speakers you can find yourself surrounded by people pronouncing Spanish words incorrectly. Then it's up to you, which pronunciation to use. (If you think this is unusual, the same thing happens with Japanese. The word "ninja" is actually pronounced "NEEN-ja", but you'll get weird looks if you do that in the US and UK, especially when referring to teenaged mutant turtles.)

Introduction

"We are painters, we paint the music with our feet"

~ Carlos Gavito

I still remember when I walked through the door to my local library and saw for the first time, a leaflet for Argentine Tango. A sole piece of jet-black cardboard, it had stark, white lettering, over a picture of two dancers sharing a moment of beauty and bliss. It stood out among all the other yellowing sheets of A4 that offered details of the local choirs and book clubs. Every time I went into that library, I'd pause for a moment and think, "Maybe..."

As fate would have it, that leaflet was from the venue where I would have my first social tango dance. While I was standing quietly, watching the dancers, I was somehow invited to dance. It was exhilarating and terrifying at the same time! I vividly remember her face against mine, and my mind going blank. I thought to myself, "Relax, breathe. Just walk and don't fall over and everything will be fine." Because honestly, right then, I didn't have any other option. With my heart racing, I couldn't even remember how to lead a basic pivot, or turn. Fortunately, no-one died, and she enjoyed it. I would later discover, that she was the best follower in the city.

And so I learned my first real lesson about getting dances. I was already "good enough". It would take me a long time to understand that lesson.

I gradually made friends at the local venues. There we would sit together and wonder how to get invitations from the "good" dancers? The consensus was, that we needed to get "good" ourselves, though no-one was entirely sure, quite what that meant.

Sometimes, we'd see someone who clearly wasn't good, managing to get dances with the better dancers, but then one of my friends would almost always explain how they were "cheating". They were young, or scantily dressed, or they were setting up their own venue and so the female teachers were just dancing with them in the hope of getting work.

I remembered that first dance and I wasn't convinced. And sometimes, when I was at another venue on my own, I'd get invited to dance by the good dancers. As far as I could tell, I wasn't cheating, but I didn't yet know what I was doing right, either.

I've always been a bit of a tango gypsy, travelling to different venues, often on my own. I enjoy dancing with people I've never met before, from all over the world, as both a leader and follower. I quickly realized I needed to find ways to get dances that didn't rely on just dancing with my friends. Unfortunately, the advice I heard was mostly contradictory. Some swore by the "cabeceo", others swore at it. Secretly, I think, back then, most had no idea what it even was.

Those who practiced different styles remarked how poor the other styles were. And yet, once in a while, people from differing styles would somehow dance, like Romeo and Juliet, and come back suitably starry-eyed about the experience. There was definitely more going on than first met the eye.

I also realized just how uncomfortable some venues could be. Looking around, I often saw a sea of awkward faces, not quite sure of what to do next, or where to put themselves. I began to see why dance cards were so popular back in the day.

At the end of each night, I wrote down in a notebook any compliments I'd received, or if I'd got to dance with any particularly notable dancers. It was a pleasant way to keep track of my progress. I'm glad I did, because this would save me over and over again, on those dark nights when nothing went right and getting dances seemed impossible, or the ones I got, were spent just painfully waiting for it to be over.

On those nights, during the drive home, I considered giving up tango. But when I finally got home, I'd pull out that notebook and read "Would you dance with my friend? I told her tango only made sense to me, after I'd danced with you" and decide, maybe, I wasn't hopeless after all.

Years passed.

I DJed a bit, ran my own small, private venue and experimented with my own ideas. While I had no desire to teach classes, I was happy to pass on advice, when asked. But I kept on hearing the same questions. How do I get to dance with that person? How do I become a better dancer, so that I can get those magical dances and people will seek me out? And I heard the same answers. Go to Buenos Aires, take this workshop, learn this style.

Yet, they never seemed to work. Sure, they'd work for a bit, but then like Icarus, the wax would melt and they'd plunge back down to where they were before. In a seemingly endless cycle, they'd dust themselves off and then try yet another workshop, teacher, or trip to Buenos Aires. Sisyphus would have been proud. A few managed to move past this stage, but they couldn't put into words **how**.

There had to be a better way.

I was, however, making progress at being comfortable in the more unwelcoming venues. I found a rich vein of ideas from psychologists, who while, frankly border-line mad scientists, were looking deeply into what makes us feel out of place and what we can do about it.

Some ideas worked, others failed, while some morphed into different and often, unexpected concepts. By now, I was regularly getting invitations with the better dancers, teachers and even the visiting superstars. Eventually I got to the point where I was consistently dancing for about a quarter, and then a third of the evening! And I was happy to enjoy listening to the music, feeling the vibe of a place, and watch people dance, for the rest of the night.

Life was good.

Years passed.

And then it all started to fall apart.

The city I was dancing in, went mad. One venue declared that they would turn up en masse, and conquer the other venues with their style. Another descended into borderline violence, as those of one style proclaimed that those who didn't, needed to be "taught a lesson". Recriminations and harsh words were spoken, both online and in the real world, with threats of physical harm being both made, and in some cases, carried out. Visiting Tango Celebrities fanned the flames, speaking of "how this was the way things were done in Buenos Aires."

While the larger styles did battle, the smaller ones became more insular. Some turned into sanctuaries, where everyone played nice. But they felt too much like children watching TV with the sound turned up, trying not to hear their parents fighting downstairs. Others even went so far as to become "private". There have always been private venues, but in the past, they were subtle about it. Now, some of their members openly taunted those not deemed "worthy" of joining, while the unworthy in turn, told anyone who would listen, how they really didn't want to go there anyway.

One night, halfway through the evening, I looked around, and instead of the beauty and bliss that had first entranced me with that simple ebony leaflet, I now saw angry faces and bodies, crashing violently around the floor. Elbows struck out and dancers collided with such abandon and force, that it resembled some kind of bizarre ice hockey match, being played out in suits and high heels.

By this time, I knew how to survive in these conditions, without needing to resort to the same. A friend and I often joked about how, at some venues, joining the dance floor was more akin to joining the Grand Melee. As the Barefoot Doctor put it, I knew how to dance with

xxiii

the fallen angels, without getting my wings mucky.

But this was different. What had begun as a misunderstood version of machismo, had twisted into something much darker. Looking out over the floor, I asked myself, did I actually want to be a part of this? I stood and watched the mayhem for a while longer, then turned and walked away.

That wintry Saturday, I found myself alone under the street-lights, looking up at the night sky, the icy wind cutting into my face, thinking, I should just give up. This is madness. There are other dances, other hobbies I could do instead.

"I'm quitting tango," I told my friend, a teacher from a different city.

"You can't quit. You need to do something to make it better!" she insisted.

I quit tango.

Or at least, I quit dancing tango socially. By this time, I was teaching teachers. My insistence on being a social dancer, rather than running my own school, meant I had accumulated a lot of insights that were hard to come by. I had no reputation to protect, no classes to sell. I didn't care if I was seen dancing with a complete beginner, or larking about with a friend. I wanted to know what really worked on the dance floor, not what looked good in a performance. And I wanted to know how you really felt comfortable in a venue, especially in the more insular ones, when you didn't know anyone there.

I wasn't a "milonguero" or a "Maestro". I was just a guy who danced.

And deep down I missed the tango I fell in love with.

One sunny afternoon, I pulled out my old notebook and read through all the compliments I'd received, remembering beautiful dances and happy followers, telling me how much they enjoyed dancing with me. I looked at the tango leaflet I'd kept from the library. Now it was faded with age, but the dancers in the photo didn't care. They were still lost in their moment together. And then I remembered that first dance...

I still talked occasionally to some in the tango community and it was clear that everyone was convinced that the trouble came from different styles. This was a "truth" I'd been told way back when I'd started and had heard countless times since. But what if they were wrong? Yes, each style had its hotheads, but they also had their fair share of lovely people. Unfortunately, right now, the hotheads were being a lot more prominent.

Help came unexpectedly. An Alexander Technique teacher had found a book I "had to read!" A retired Tiller Girl, she kept meaning to take up tango, but in the meantime, had taken to living vicariously through me. The book explained how people looked at the world very differently from each other. Some, like the Bonobo monkeys, felt that a life well lived, was one where you shared with those around you. The most respected Bonobo monkeys were those who were skilled at foraging and then gave a share of their bananas to the weaker and smaller members of the tribe.

Whereas the Great Apes were Darwinian in their approach, feeling that you were responsible for getting your own bananas and indeed that a clear hierarchy was necessary to keep things working smoothly.

An idea began to flicker into life.

What if tango attracted its own cooperative Bonobo monkeys and competitive Great Apes? Would that better explain what was going on? Certainly a lot of tango dancers fitted into those two boxes, but there were still pieces missing.

I looked back over all the people I met, the places I'd been, the dances I'd had, the unobtainable partners, and I started to see other patterns emerge. Gradually, they coalesced into two more types. I talked to friends and teachers about my theories to see if they matched their experiences as well.

And then I went back to tango.

The storm had passed. But not without cost. A great many dancers had left, and unlike me, most wouldn't return. Several of the warring venues had collapsed, unable to maintain themselves under the weight of all the in-fighting. Those that remained, had no appetite to see tango wiped out. And so calmer heads had eventually prevailed.

Talking to people afterwards, I came to see how so much of it really hadn't been about styles at all. Great Apes on all sides had arrived from other countries, and riled up the indigenous apes in my city. Together they rampaged through the tango forest, trying to enforce their way on everyone else, loudly beating their chests and threatening anyone not of their troop. This sent the Bonobos and others into hiding, until the instigating Apes finally returned to their own countries. Mercifully, without their influence, those that remained, eventually grew exhausted and calmed down.

I had no interest in joining "sides". I wanted to get back to blissful dances again. But with my new-found insight, everything became much clearer. I started looking at the ways the different types behaved. What did you need to do to get a dance with each? And what would sink your chances? If you offered your bananas freely, would the Great Ape be offended, or would the Bonobo hug you with delight?

Gradually, I polished the ideas, seeing what worked and what didn't, revealing the subtle nuances. Until finally, I realized I could go into any milonga and enjoy blissful dances for the entire evening.

Now the days of dancing a third of the time are long gone. These days, the only reason I'm not dancing all the time, is if I chose not to.

I finally understand that first lesson. I was always good enough. The difference is, now I know how to enjoy getting the dances I want! While the Great Ape in me, who thinks you should have to figure this out on your own, is being kept distracted by the other two, the Bonobo side of me offers this book to you and hopes you get lots of enjoyable dances of your own. Let's begin by taking a closer look at the four types of tango dancers.

Chapter 1 - How do I get to dance with that person?

"Imagine I put two glasses of water in front of you. One will make you better at dancing tango, the other will make you better at getting the dances you want, and you can drink both. Which one would you drink first?"

I asked this to a friend as I was writing the first draft of this book. She wanted the glass that would make her better at gaining the partners she wanted, so I've written this book first. The second glass will be covered in later books.

There are people who are unattractive, overweight, sweaty, old, and really bad at tango to the point of being painful to dance with, and yet they *still* have plenty of willing partners. The worst dancer I know is profoundly irritating and definitely not getting dances based on his looks. Just watching his technique makes many others wince. Yet he has a constant stream of beautiful partners who are lovely people. However, one of the best dancers I know is very attractive, and a lovely person with impeccable technique and connection, and yet she struggles to get invited to dance.

So what's going on?

When talking about this, a question that comes up a lot is variations on "What are you looking for in a dance partner?" Such as,

"What is it about the way a follower dances that makes you pick her, or indeed cross her off your list? Is being young, hot and forgetting to finish getting dressed, really all that's needed? Do adornments catch the eye of the discerning leader?"

A specific answer I've given in the past was,

"Ok, well, she looks totally relaxed. Completely 'in the moment'. There's no ambiguity, or hesitation. She's dancing."

And so, understandably, a lot of followers think that if they can discover The List Of What Makes An Irresistible Follower and tick off everything on it, then they'll be inundated with the dances they want. Of course, that still wouldn't get rid of those pesky, young, hot women who keep getting dances they clearly don't deserve...

Likewise, what is it that makes the irresistible leader? Is it musicality, the perfect embrace *(the way the partners hold each other in the dance)*, or a repertoire of moves worthy of a Broadway Show?

Or maybe, you think that paying to go to a milonga in itself entitles you to a certain amount of dancing?

There are a lot of different perspectives.

Unfortunately, nothing fails like success. Just because the people who will dance with anyone are happy to accept your invitation, doesn't mean you couldn't do better if you tried to invite the people who are a bit fussier. Or maybe you should start with the easiest partners and systematically work your way up the food chain? Perhaps you should only focus on the people who are crazy about you?

So what should you do? One thing's for sure, this is a subject that causes a lot of pain and confusion.

The good news is, despite what you probably think, no-one is completely unobtainable, regardless of who you are and how "good" you think you are. The bad news is, you've probably been asking the wrong question. It turns out your question isn't really "How do I get a dance with them?" It's "How do I get a dance with them, *using the methods I'm comfortable with?"*

Those few extra words complicate things a lot. Sometimes to succeed, you're going to have to do something you really don't like. I don't necessarily mean mass murder, and what makes you uncomfortable depends very much on who you are. Some blanch at the idea of turning down a beginner who's gotten up the courage to ask. Some don't want to join a clique, while others are happy to do so.

Think about this for a moment, because it can send you into a tailspin of seemingly endless frustration.

Imagine trying to start a new, expensive car that doesn't have any gas in the tank, by taking lessons on how to improve the way you put it in gear. That car isn't going anywhere, no matter how fluid your control of the clutch! On the other hand, someone else may only have an old, beaten up, second-hand car and barely be able to drive it without grinding the gears, but if they've put gas in it, they can at least get it to move.

For example, let's say that the person you want to invite, absolutely refuses to dance with people who aren't in their group, and right now, you're not a member. In this case, it simply doesn't matter how much you refine your technique, they won't accept your invitation. On the other hand, someone with much less skill than you, but who is a member of their group, may well be able to get dances with them. They have gas, but you don't.

This is one of those cases where the rabbit hole goes really deep. If you haven't already, feel free to get something to drink before reading the rest of this.

Down the Rabbit Hole

It's commonly assumed that the more experienced dancers are far out of the beginners' reach. The reason for that tends to have less to do with beginners' actual dancing skills, and more that they often use beginner strategies when trying to get dances.

This doesn't just apply to beginners by the way. If you don't improve the way in which you get dances, you can eventually end up in the miserable position of being "advanced", but unable to invite the partners you want. Likewise, those "beginners", who may, or may not be young, hot and scantily-clad, who are snaffling up all the desirable partners, could have picked up those advanced social skills from their life before tango. Maybe from a previous style of dance? Perhaps it just comes naturally to them? Or it could be any one of a hundred other things that mean they already know how to do it, and they know how to do it very well.

To understand the dynamics at play here, let's look at the different 'tribes' that inhabit the milongas.

A lot of the misery that comes from the social side of tango stems from assuming that everyone else views the world the way that you do, or thinking that if they don't, then they should do.

Broadly speaking, you can break tango dancers down into four different types. Unfortunately, tactics that work with one can backfire horribly when used with another. The four types are Competitive, Cooperative, Nurturing and Free Spirits.

Competitive dancers

Competitive dancers view milongas as a meritocracy. They measure how good they are by the skill of the people who chose to invite them. While they want to dance with the best, sometimes this means they won't ask people who are much better than them, because they don't consider themselves worthy yet and don't want to be Found Out To Not Be Good Enough. They can also feel that things should be Done A Certain Way. It's often important to them not to be seen with someone significantly "beneath" them, as this lowers their perceived value and encourages unwanted invitations.

A Competitive teacher, for example, is probably not going to dance socially with the beginners. They're probably not even going to dance with you socially, unless you're a close friend or a teacher yourself.

It's not unusual for Competitive dancers to form groups (often referred to as cliques or Harems, by those dancers who aren't members) in their local venues, to actively keep other the dancers there from approaching them. When better opportunities present themselves, such as a visiting teacher that they respect, or when they find themselves in a Bigger Pond, like a Festival, they'll often try to seize them.

Competitive venues are likely to have a constant supply of high-end guest teachers who will give classes based around difficult sequences of moves and then never see you again, unless you do their workshops.

Some Competitive dancers feel that the end justifies the means. They crash into people, swerve around all over the place and so on, because it's part of the "learning process". Some also adopt the attitude that it is only right, that lesser dancers should get out of their way. This mindset can be tempered, when enough dancers agree that Doing Things The Right Way includes proper floorcraft.

Competitive dancers are consistent in the way they invite potential partners. This is part of Doing It Properly. What this means exactly can vary a lot. But often they prefer the cabeceo (cah-beh-SAY-oh – *non-verbal method of asking for dances, see Chapter 5 for more information*) as a method of filtering potential partners.

Typical quote - *"I've never heard anything bad about her teaching, only that she used to dance well, but no longer does, because she no longer dances socially with anyone who dances well. I've danced with her once (her leading) and thought she was perfectly OK, given the style, and music, and also a very nice and intelligent person. I haven't danced with enough of her students to say anything about the results she gets. And it's not the dance I prefer, it can't really achieve that floaty feeling and isn't aimed at doing so, so I'm probably not the person to say. She surely knows what she's talking about."*

"I only have to say 'No!', once!" - Lexi Taylor

Cooperative dancers

Cooperative dancers want harmony throughout the milonga and believe that the means justifies the end. They view how good they are by how much everyone in the venue has a good time. Community is important to them. This is exemplified by the kind of milonga where the teachers dance with a wide range of people, often in both roles. They don't restrict themselves to just the Chosen Few, their partner, or other teachers.

There's a greater likelihood of it being acceptable to verbally invite partners. It's considered perfectly normal for the most experienced to be dancing with those who just did the Beginner's class. Cooperative Dancers make an effort to dance with everyone. If they miss someone out, it's not unusual for them to say, "Hi" afterwards to make it clear they weren't snubbing them.

Some people even have complicated algorithms and flowcharts in their heads to make sure that they dance with as many people as possible. The overall idea is you all play nice and everyone goes home happy. If you've ever been to a party where everyone was asked to bring along some food and drink to share, you've got the idea.

Venues that follow this ethos, are places where everyone knows your name. The people who go there tend to be nice and will usually cut their friends a bit of slack. Bumps are nodded off in better humor, they're more likely to let you into the ronda *(RON-dah - the flow of dancers cooperating and dancing together in harmony as they gradually move anti-clockwise around the room, generally without changing lanes)* and so on. It's normal to be introduced to others and indeed experience both sides of "Would you dance with my friend?"

Rather than bring in one-off superstars, often the organizer also teaches and in a way that encourages harmony in the ronda. The códigos *(CO-dee-gohs — a code of conduct for the milonga, which varies from venue to venue)* are also designed for everyone's benefit. Birthday valses, *(VAL-ses — a vals, singular, is one of the styles of music that tango is danced to. For more information on Birthday valses, see Chapter 10.)* are common, as are ways of including people who are new or being left out, such as the followers' tanda, where the followers ask the leaders. It takes true determination to not get a dance in these venues.

Cooperative dancers don't want anyone to feel uncomfortable. In a Cooperative venue, they'll come over and say, "Hi", or someone will introduce them. It will be obvious that they're happy to see you and want to make you feel welcome. Don't expect elaborate cabeceo rituals here.

A really simple method for getting dances in a Cooperative venue is to do the class before the milonga and talk to everyone you partner with (though not while the teacher is trying to explain something!) Now you've got a good pool to dance with later on and who will introduce you to others during the milonga.

Typical quote - *"It's so good to see you here. Have you met....?"*

Nurturing dancers

Nurturing dancers will look out for people who are on the same wavelength as them. It might be a specific style, or in their outlook towards tango. Either way, they're happy to invest time and energy in them. They measure how good they are by their partner, particularly by how much they improve. They're comfortable dancing multiple tandas with the same person, attending workshops together, and so forth. Unfortunately, this sometimes goes wrong when the leader isn't as good as they think they are and rather than actually leading, start expecting the follower to develop telepathy. One such leader once proudly told me "I wouldn't dream of leading her." They tend to gravitate towards prácticas (PRAC-tee-cas - *practice sessions)* and milongas where there's enough space to be able to stop and explain things. Choosing their partners is important to them, so they are more likely to avoid Cooperative venues.

They can sometimes find better dancers of either role intimidating at first. But after several years they often see that the "better dancers" are all just ordinary people after all.

In a Nurturing práctica, it's left to the dancers to go and ask the teacher for advice, or simply work it out between themselves. Bringing along music to experiment with is often encouraged and there's usually plenty of room.

Because Nurturers tend to know their preferred partners well, they will often sit together and chat as they get changed into their dance shoes. The main thing they ask of a venue is that they can be left in peace to dance with who they want for as much as they want.

Typical quote - *"It's not so much the ones who want a bit of a social life - I think they can be worked on to be good enough social dancers [in theory]. It's the fantasists that trouble me - the ones who imagine they are wowing us with their schlocky imitations of show dancing and therefore have the right to mess up the ronda or prance about in the middle."*

"Sisterhood - I do try to engender it whenever possible. I think many of those haughty entitled tango vixens are actually brazening it out and just occasionally a friendly word can help them move on from it. The sort of Competitive tactics that are all too familiar hardly reflect true confidence or a relaxed state of mind. There are some lovely tango women out there - kind, friendly, thoughtful and great fun to be around. It's a sad thought there are people who will never take the time to get to know them and see them only as competition."

Free Spirit dancers

Free Spirits will ask whoever is nearest and looks like they'd be enjoyable to dance with. They're the magpies of tango, always chasing the nearest shiny. They are often, quite simply, a Force of Nature. They measure how good they are by how much they can enjoy the night. They don't have any real strategies for getting dances, other than being friendly and often mischievous. Trying to figure out their strategy is like looking for meaning in clouds. Yes, you'll see that this cloud looks like a castle and that one a dragon, but the meaning is only in your head and it will slowly change shape or disappear before your eyes.

On the dance floor, anything goes. They delight in creating and exploring new possibilities, often fusing together elements from other dances or arts and seeing what happens.

A Free Spirit invites people to play with them in whatever seems the most direct, enjoyable way. Anything from pulling faces, to running up and giving you a hug.

Free Spirit venues tend to be chaotic, but friendly. The organizer may give a shout-out to visiting groups to make them feel welcome. Birthday valses (Chapter 10) are a lively celebration of madness. Despite, or perhaps, because of the chaos, and undeterred by nuevo *(nu-AY-vo – a style of dancing, a teaching methodology and a genre of tango music)* dancers' reputation for being scythe-wielding psychopaths, Free Spirit venues often have surprisingly good floorcraft.

Typical quote - *"Wooooooooooooooooohoooooooooooooooooo!"* - 'Lucia'

What is it that you really want right now?

Having read those descriptions, which did you find yourself nodding to? Not what other people tell you it should be, but what *you* really want? The more honest you are with yourself about this, the easier it will be. Likewise, which descriptions did you find yourself shaking your head at?

Being in a milonga that doesn't match your type can cause you problems. For example, a Cooperative venue may well actively introduce a follower to the various leaders there, rather than letting them decide who to approach or cabeceo. This is going to make a Cooperative dancer happy, but it's going to drive a Competitive dancer insane. Conversely, the owners of a Competitive milonga are far more likely to sit by and do nothing, even if someone has clearly not managed to get any dances for the entire night, which will please the Competitive dancers, but annoy the Cooperative ones. So generally, you're going to be happier in a place that's the same as you.

There are a few exceptions to this. If you're looking for Nurturing dancers, you may only need a few of them to be able to dance most of the night. In which case it doesn't really matter what types the rest of the people there are composed of, provided you can cope with the floorcraft without getting flustered and that neither of you feel pressured to dance with other people.

If you're Competitive, get yourself into a Competitive group and voilà.

If you're Cooperative, you're probably going to need a venue with a reasonable number of like-minded people.

And if you're a Free Spirit, pretty much you just need somewhere that won't throw you out for breaking all their Rules and that has a reasonable number of people you like the look of who will dance with you.

You may find that you feel like you don't always belong to the same types. It can change throughout the same evening, or vary at different events or venues, or according to your moods, states of mind or company, etc. Some seemingly Competitive types will think of themselves as Nurturing within their selected circle, or as Cooperative if they organize or promote an event, or even as Free-Spirited if their guard slips and they find themselves not only dancing with an Unknown but enjoying it...

Why tango, as a whole, isn't a meritocracy

Simply put, most of the people who think tango is a meritocracy, are Competitive dancers and they're only in the majority at specific venues. This means that the Competitive dancers who think tango should be a meritocracy are in a minority overall. They do however, have a tendency to be vocal. Also, rather importantly, all four types are represented amongst the "good" dancers.

There's an overarching culture of fear in tango that encourages people to buy these shoes, do that workshop, go to Buenos Aires, so that eventually you'll earn the right to invite the more experienced. In large part, this is because tango has taken a lot of its business model from Salsa which is not generally known for its warmth and inclusivity!

This in turn, leads to insane situations. I remember a young woman in a red dress at a milonga that was renowned for its Good Dancers. She looked like the archetypal young, hot, inexperienced woman. She was with her boyfriend, who, as far as I could tell, had done one class and was very uncomfortable with the whole situation. He was however, doing his best and had reasonable floorcraft. She clearly adored him and did her best to follow his fumbling leading. No-one wanted to ask her to dance, because they didn't want to be seen as That Guy who invites a beginner, just because she's young and hot.

After a while I got annoyed. I don't have any issue dancing with beginners anyway, but she was clearly a decent human being. She wasn't ditching her boyfriend in an attempt to get better dances. If anything, she was helping him keep it together, in what was clearly a stressful situation for him. And people can think whatever they like about me. So I invited her and it became obvious that despite her age and looks, she was a good follower. At which point, the other leaders suddenly had a moment of realization and started offering her invitations of their own.

So it's not always all sunshine and rainbows for the young, hot women after all. It's worth noting that despite the sudden influx of invitations, she continued to alternate dancing tandas with her boyfriend (who sadly did not receive any interest from the other followers and I doubt my offering to follow him would have helped!) and continued sitting some tandas out and keeping him company. By the end of the night, I had a lot more respect for the two of them than I did for the other leaders.

The idea that because you're young and good looking, you must be terrible at dancing, never made any sense to me anyway. "Beginners" can have skills that are independent of their time spent in tango, such as posture and connection, that make a big difference to their following and that far more experienced followers don't necessarily have. Likewise, "experienced" just means you've spent a fair amount of time and energy dancing tango. That doesn't mean you've got anywhere useful.

A large motivation for my writing these books came from realizing that many dancers tend to get stuck in the intermediate stage and then just go round and round in circles, trying new ideas, taking private lessons and so forth, but rarely making any real progress when it comes to social dancing, particularly at getting invitations from "better" dancers.

There's plenty of people who you may consider "out of your reach" who would be quite happy to dance with you, provided you take the right   approach.

Chapter 2 - What am I doing wrong?

"Dance with him. Go on. He's not dancing with anyone and he's in a

good mood. Go on!"

* afterwards*

"How was it?"

Pulls a disappointed face

It's easy to get an incomplete model in your head. To get caught up thinking that people who are "good", or dance a certain way, or who are DJs etc, are the people you want to dance with. But there's usually other factors involved too and by ignoring them, you can frustrate yourself. A lot! In life, we tend to create mental shortcuts, because frankly it takes too long to figure out every situation from scratch. But in tango they can cause us problems, so we end up like Sisyphus, forever pushing the rock up the mountain, only to have it roll all the way back down, just as we reach the top.

"Everyone called Sally is female. All women are female. Therefore, all women are called Sally." It's logical, but unfortunately it's also wrong.

Let's say you know you only want to dance with women called Sally (where "women called Sally" means whatever it is you're looking for in a partner) and you see someone who's a woman. Instead of thinking, "This looks promising. I should find out if her name is Sally" you think "She's a woman and so must be Sally! I want to dance with her." Only it turns out, she's called Beth and the dances you then have together are horrible.

It's remarkable how easy it is to fall into these traps, especially if you're not taking into account the four types. (And no, I haven't even got into the quagmire of different styles yet!) Think about the last time you wanted to dance with someone at a milonga and in some way, they turned you down? Most people's first reaction is to beat themselves up over this and make a Big Deal about being rejected.

But ask yourself, why did you want to dance with them in the first place? Presumably because either you thought you'd enjoy it, or perhaps you thought you'd learn from the experience. The problem is it's surprisingly easy to shift from thinking "this might be enjoyable", to acting as if you can predict the future and you know with certainty that it will be.

Something I hear a lot is "I want to get to dance with them, because they're good." But if that person's definition of "good" is how it feels to dance with them, then because they haven't danced with them yet, they don't know what it feels like to dance with them. So they don't actually know if that person is good!

What if instead, you'd thought "I'd like to try them out and see. Maybe they're good, maybe not?" And if the person turned you down, you just accepted it. You haven't lost anything, because you didn't know what it was going to be like. Maybe they're tense, drunk and in an awful mood and the three or four dances of that tanda would have been the worst fifteen minutes of your life, leaving you physically injured and unable to dance for a month. Suddenly, rather than being rejected, this person has spared you from a horrible experience.

Aha! But what if you've danced with them before and you know they're a good dancer? Well, if they're tense, drunk and in an awful mood, you're still back to the same answer. Just because something worked one way in the past, doesn't mean it's going to work that way now, especially with dancing. I'm exaggerating for clarity, but bear in mind there's a lot that effects people's dancing that isn't really obvious just from looking at them.

How about if you only wanted to dance with people to get the experience in order to improve? On face value, it makes sense to dance with people above your level, gradually getting better and in doing so, get to dance with increasingly better people. You can then objectively tell how well you're doing by who chooses to dance with you (rather than who you can coerce!) But in tango, "better" is remarkably subjective. The simple fact that you think someone is better than you, means you don't completely understand why they are. You're assuming that dancing with them is a Good Thing.

Dancing with better dancers won't make you a better dancer, it will (potentially) make you better at dancing with better dancers, which is not quite the same thing.

Which would be fine if you were psychic and could see the future. Instead, what often happens is that someone eventually gets to dance with a "better" dancer and is delighted. For roughly three to six months. But then they may find they've outgrown them. So far, not a problem, they just move onto the next better dancer, right? Unfortunately, what also often happens is they realize that they've picked up some bad habits from dancing with that person that they didn't have before. They now have to unlearn those habits. Given they just spent about half a year ingraining those habits, that's probably not a problem they're going to fix overnight.

How the different Types frustrate each other

It can be particularly annoying if you're using techniques that would successfully work with your type and in doing so, are repelling those of different types who you want to dance with. Let's take a look at the way the various types drive each other insane. My aim isn't to convince you that any one type is right or wrong. Just that the people in the other types are doing things for reasons that make sense to them. They're not evil and trying to ruin your night. But it's also crazy-making trying to interact with them as if they were a member of your type, or trying to convince them that they should behave that way.

Competitive dancers

Competitive dancers are unusual in that they manage to annoy all the types, including other Competitive dancers. They mainly accomplish this by being cautious of who they dance with, especially strangers, preferring to watch them first and sometimes ask other's about them. This is simply baffling to Cooperative and Free Spirits, who tend to view them as stuck-up, haughty hotshots, looking down their noses at everyone else. Even Nurturers can get irritated at Competitive dancers continually judging them and trying to get them to join their group, especially if the Nurturer is only interested in dancing with one person in that group.

Psychologists have found that humans feel twice as bad from a loss, as the same gain makes them feel good. So, if for example, I offer to flip a coin and I'll give you $10 if it lands on heads, but if it lands on tails you have to give me $7, most people won't do it. It needs to drop to you giving me less than $5 if you lose, before most people will even consider it. That's a BIG factor, especially for someone in a group to risk dancing with someone outside of it, because normally, the likelihood of dancing with them being a "win" has to be at least twice as much as it being a "loss", causing them to be much more risk adverse.

Let's take a look at Carl. Carl views himself as "experienced" and has adopted the following system – if you want to dance with him, he first has to see you dancing with Connor, Cody or Charles. However, if at any point he sees you dancing with Edward, Emile or Eric it's all over, do not collect $200 and he's unavailable to you for the rest of the milonga.

It's worth considering what's going on here. You might want to use it yourself and even if you don't, it'll help you see why Carl and people like him, aren't necessarily stuck-up hotshots. During the milonga, Carl sees you (a follower) on the dance floor with Connor. First of all, he trusts Connor's ability to filter out the people neither of them are interested in. Then he can ask Connor afterwards what you were like? (The most frequent question men ask each other about followers in my experience is "What was she like to dance with?") Likewise, if you really messed up with Connor, he's most likely going to go and complain to the other leaders in the group about it! So at a simple level, it's just a way of filtering. This also works if you're a leader trying to get a dance with a Competitive follower.

The other problem is that if you belong to a group and you dance with someone outside the group, particularly if they're considered to be "not good enough", that can give the people who were being filtered out, ideas about inviting the other members after all.

In the above example, if Carl dances with Mary who's considered "beneath" the group, then Maggie and Molly who consider themselves to be as good as Mary, might now consider asking Carl and the other members of the group too, such as Connor and Cody. Connor and Cody will not be happy bunnies if this happens.

What this means is that if you want to dance with someone in a group, without joining it, you're now contending with the whole group dynamic, and not just the one person you want to dance with. This is extremely annoying if you don't even like the rest of the group!

Competitive groups usually have a vetting process, particularly if there are a limited number of places available. If you want to join, look for the person in charge of the vetting. Surprisingly, they're often not the Top Dogs. Look for someone lower down the totem pole that's willing to talk to you, and make nice to them. Don't be pushy. Gently show that you agree with the ethos of the group.

"This is {insert your name here}, the one I was telling you about" - is worth its weight in gold as an introduction to groups. Likewise, often getting a private lesson with the Right Teacher, or being friends with the right DJ or Organizer, can get you a temporary pass to the group. Once you're in, if you want to stay in, try to pick up on the buzzwords and in-jokes that they use. It might be musicality, mocking people who dance in a certain way, or having certain views on the cabeceo. It could be references to "that time at the pizza after-party" and the merriment that was had seeing how high it was possible to stack the empty pizza boxes.

However, also be aware that it can be a pyramid scheme, so you may need to pay your dues and gradually work your way up. Having said that, people who are drawn to Competitive groups tend to like there being a structure in place that they can systematically advance through. They can positively enjoy the struggle and indeed may quit if they ever reach the top, preferring instead to leave in search of new pursuits with which to challenge themselves.

Have a look at where the money and the power are going. Does the group have an Authority on how to dance? Do they go to or run workshops and Festivals (see Chapter 12) for more information) that you'll be expected to regularly attend? Especially look out for situations where the give and take isn't even. If the Authority wants to stay at your place for free while they're in the country for the weekend, do you get something equal in return, other than the pleasure of their company?

Perhaps strangely, it's not a problem in and of itself, if there isn't give and take. If the Authority spends most of their time in another country, but their existence holds the group together, that's a good thing if you want to be a part of that group. If they've any sense, the Festivals and workshops will be useful and/or enjoyable to the people in the group, which includes you. The people who went, really did enjoy stacking those pizza boxes! Just make sure you know what you're getting yourself into, or at least find out as soon as possible. Tango can run into thousands of dollars and voraciously eat up free time that you might want to spend with friends, family, hobbies, or simply sleep! It can also be heart-breaking to find yourself left out, because you don't have enough spare time or money.

Also, be wary when you don't know for sure what the end experience is going to be like. You're going to need a source of sufficiently good partners to enjoy yourself. People leave tango. They move, have children, some of them even die. If your circle keeps shrinking, you may end up with no-one left to dance with. Which is a lousy ending, for years of hard work.

There's an innate paradox to the Competitive model. Let's go back to the magic glasses of water from the beginning of Chapter 1 ? If I offer them to a Nurturer, they'll ask for some more to share with their partner(s). Whereas a Cooperative dancer will want to arrange some kind of mass distribution system so that everyone can benefit and have more enjoyment from tango. A Free Spirit will be quite happy to let someone *else* organize the mass distribution system! But a Competitive dancer is going to think twice about letting other dancers know about this. Why help your competition, especially if you see them as the enemy?

It goes deeper than that. This model attracts people for whom the greater the struggle, the greater the value of each achievement. Likewise, the fewer people who have accomplished something, the more valuable it is. By not Nurturing and Cooperating with each other, the journey takes a lot longer and is a lot more arduous. Provided that you actually agree with this, that's fine. If you don't, but now realize that you've been pulled into a Competitive environment, then you might want to take some time and reflect about what it is you really want and how you want to get it.

It's also worth bearing in mind, that when you look at the "Experienced", all four types are represented. Becoming good, doesn't mean that you have to join a Competitive group and systematically work your way up the food chain.

How to approach Competitives

- Find the person who'll invite you into the group.

- Learn to make the right noises and go to the right places.

- A private lesson with the relevant person can get you an in.

- Only dance with the "right" people.

- Always accept "No" for an answer gracefully.

- Do things the "right" way (according to them).

- Don't assume that dancing with them in one venue means they'll dance with you in another.

Cooperative dancers

Cooperative Dancers tend to wreak havoc with the other types because of their belief that everyone should talk to and dance with each other. Meanwhile, all the other types want to be able to chose who they dance and socialize with, though for very different reasons. By cheerfully dancing with people "beneath" themselves, they break the Competitive dancer's meritocracy. Competitive dancers also do not welcome the idea that they too should have to dance with everyone.

Nurturers usually dislike being expected to mingle, and would rather dance all night with their chosen partner(s). And Free Spirits have no interest in keeping track of who they dance with, or being told to share the love, so that no-one feels left out.

On the bright side, Cooperative dancers tend to be very open and friendly. Because of this, sometimes the other types will deliberately seek them out, either for warm-up dances earlier on before the people they want to dance with arrive, or just to get over a rough patch, especially if they've fallen out of favor with their current group or partner, or their favorite venue is closed. This can then cause confusion for Cooperative dancers who are getting invitations from the other types at Cooperative venues, but then suddenly find themselves apparently invisible when they're elsewhere.

Competitive dancers often feel that there is no drive for Cooperative dancers to improve, as they can simply get the dances they want at their venues by saying "Hello" and asking. Some Cooperative dancers simply aren't interested in getting beyond the point where they can have a fun night out. However, others progress to high standards and tend to be versatile and able to adapt, often being able to dance both roles.

How to approach Cooperatives

- Go to a Cooperative Venue and play nice.
- Say "Hi" and smile a lot.
- Get someone to introduce you.
- If you're not in a Cooperative Venue, being friendly will still usually work, as they're more likely to see you as a kindred spirit, compared to the other "hostile" non-sharing dancers.
- See Chapter 6 for advice on talking to strangers

Nurturers

Nurturers can drive Competitive dancers insane. As one Competitive follower put it, "they mess up the economics of the milonga." When a Nurturer dances with one partner, sometimes called "hogging them", for most of the evening, Competitive dancers feel that they only get the leftover tandas, rather than being able to choose the tanda by an Orchestra that would have inspired them both. They are also unable to "earn" the right to dance with Nurturing dancers, as they make their choices more on personal compatibility, rather than technical skill. Competitive partners, especially women, often disliked being "hogged" and can be very concerned about other potential partners thinking they are in a relationship with the Nurturer and so are "off-limits", further disrupting the economics of the situation.

Cooperative dancers may also be annoyed with the "unfairness" of someone spending so much time with their own partner and not sharing their dances out evenly, because other people are then forced to sit out and have their feelings hurt.

Nurturers feel that everyone's free to be with whoever they chose, as often as they want. It's worth bearing in mind, that usually, had they not come intending to dance together, they simply wouldn't have come at all and so really, the presence of a Nurturing couple has no effect on anyone else in the milonga. Ironically, they may accept a few dances with other people, which wouldn't have happened if they'd decided to stay at home instead.

Let's say that Jack and Jill are a Nurturing couple. On the first week of February, they both decided to go to a Cooperative milonga together and only danced with each other. On the second week, Jill wanted to go, but Jack didn't, complaining about not feeling up to it, after falling down a hill. So Jill stayed at home as well and they watched a dvd and ate pizza. The only difference between those two nights for the other people who turned up to the milonga, was that on the first night, the Organizer made slightly more money (which helps to keep the venue running, the people who aren't dancing with you, are still contributing to the costs of the milonga you're enjoying) and throughout the evening there was one extra couple either on the dance floor, or sitting down. That's it.

On the third week, Jack's not quite better, but Jill really wants to go, so they go along again. This time, Jack's sitting out a bit more, so Jill does dance a few tandas with other people. This time, they've both contributed to the costs of the night and there are now some opportunities to dance with Jill, which wouldn't have been there had they both stayed at home. To a Nurturer, this all makes perfect sense.

How to approach Nurturers

- Be yourself. This is all about syncing up as dancers.
- If you want to dance with them in the long term, show a genuine interest in getting better that syncs up with what they want.
- Some like to talk, others prefer to message, about finding better ways to do things. These conversations can last for years.
- Going to a practica and asking them for advice can also work.

Free Spirits

Free Spirits are baffled by Competitive partners' insistence on doing things like the cabeceo "The Right Way". Likewise, Free Spirits will choose those who are shiny and enjoyable. Which is definitely not the same thing as technically skilled and dogmatic. So while the Competitive dancer may feel that they're more than good enough to get an invitation from the Free Spirit, if all the Free Spirit sees is a grey cloud of gloom, fixated on making sure proper etiquette is observed, and focused on exact technique, rather than connection and fun, then the Free Spirit will probably look elsewhere.

Those in the Competitive type tend to feel once they've danced with a "good" partner, whether they can consistently get them again is a measure of their skill. Free Spirits don't do consistency. To make things worse, they will cheerfully invite people who are "beneath them", potentially encouraging those partners to then ask the Competitive dancer!

Free Spirits can also infuriate Cooperative types, by their randomness in whom they chose. Going up to them and saying "You didn't dance with me tonight" won't work, because they'll have forgotten you said it in about a minute's time.

When you're dancing with a Free Spirit, but the only person enjoying themselves is you, they're unlikely to ask you again in the future.

How to approach Free Spirits

- Don't approach getting dances with Free Spirits logically. You have to take a more emotional approach.
- Free Spirits tend to be empathic, so you want them to feel that dancing with you will be a "shiny happy" experience.

- Do your thing as long as you don't look like a cloud of doom or boredom.

- When you're dancing, don't worry about making mistakes. Get into the habit of smiling if you mess up, rather than saying "sorry".

- They're also notoriously playful, so again a willingness to play is a good thing. You can convey this to them by the way you dance with other people, and how you talk to them – stick to upbeat positive conversation.

- Don't take whether they dance with you tonight personally.

Practising recognising the Types online

Look at any online discussion of tango and it will suddenly make much more sense once you realize the four types are practically talking different languages to each other. The Competitive posters will be telling people the "Right" way to do things, often saying "In BsAs they...", or how they learned the correct way from a famous teacher (usually in BsAs!) Their points are black and white, and rarely open to change. They're telling you the answer and waiting for you to agree and thank them.

Nurturers will be trying, usually in vain, to find a better answer. This tends to annoy the Competitives who feel that their answer doesn't need any improving and especially not from someone who isn't a master from BsAs. Nurturers will keep trying to drag the thread back on topic, often giving up and starting a new thread, or carrying on the conversation privately.

Cooperatives will make innocuous comments that shouldn't offend anyone. They're often happiest on the "Yay! Look at all the photos, wasn't it a wonderful time" threads, or any thread that has "appreciation" in the title. They may attempt to bring peace to a thread that's beginning to show signs of getting aggressive, but will leave if they feel directly attacked and may chose to simply "lurk" in the future.

Free Spirits will derail a thread almost instantly by ignoring the actual topic and talking about something else entirely, possibly not even related to tango. They are completely irreverent, but this can lead them to trolling, which they consider harmless, because "it's not real and it's all meant in good fun".

The four Types discuss tango online

Nurturer "I'm trying to find a better way to do ochos in open embrace. I feel like the follower keeps stepping away from me and I don't know how to solve this. Does anyone have any suggestions?"

Competitive "You shouldn't be doing ochos in open embrace anyway. Just learn to do them in close, the way they do in BsAs. When I was there, I never saw anyone dancing in open."

Cooperative "I quite like dancing in both open or close embrace. As long as we both enjoy it, everything's good :) :) :) "

Nurturer "Yes, I understand that, but I want to solve this problem specifically."

Free Spirit "Angelina Jolie was sooooooooooooo hot last night. Can't wait till tomorrow's episode. Oh and SPOILERS, Helen dies."

Competitive "You're wasting your time learning to dance in open. Look I can recommend some teachers who specialize in a proper BsAs close embrace if you want?"

Cooperative "When I was dancing at the Happy Festival, lots of people were dancing in open and I had some lovely dances with them :) :) :) "

Competitive "Yes, well, we all know the kind of people who go to the Happy Festival. In BsAs, they'd already be dead!"

Cooperative - This User has deleted their account -

Free Spirit "I mean a head shot from a mile! I really didn't see that coming. Well neither did Helen :p "

Nurturer "This thread is going nowhere, I'm going to restart it at this link*"*

Free Spirit "Meh, I bet Angelina could kill all of you!"

Changing Types

A caveat, people change, just because they're not interested in inviting you now, doesn't mean they won't be in the future. And this isn't the "get better and people will choose you" meme. The way people approach tango gradually changes over time. A bad fit now, may be a great fit in the future. Similarly, the more someone wants to dance with you, the more energy there is to magnify – this is where great moments come from!

But can't you convince anyone that your type is the Right One for them too? First ask yourself, what would it take to change your mind that their type is the right one for you? Suddenly the question got a lot harder. Likewise, even if you have changed your mind from one type to another in the past, that was what worked for you at that point in time. Don't expect the same revelation to work for necessarily someone else.

Chapter 3 - Finding the Right Venues for you

"Oh, how I wish I had only to travel 100 miles for tango... Here, I'd have to go some 400 miles for a practica. On a Wednesday evening. In a town smaller than my own. No tango here for miles and miles and miles.

And so we cry."

~ Bridget Michlig

Now that you know which type you are and what you want, how can you find suitable venues? Start by having a look at the websites, advertising and Social Media Pages of various milongas. Look at the posts of people who regularly attend. You can even simply ask people who go there to describe it. That should give you a good idea of the venue itself, the overall composition of types and what those specific people are like. For example, a Cooperative venue may still have a few Free Spirits who turn up regularly and a fixed couple of Nurturing dancers.

At this point, hopefully you have some milongas that you think might suit you. In which case, great, go ahead and try them. But if there aren't a lot of milongas, particularly if you live somewhere that isn't near a major city, then it may come down to trying to find the least worst option. Yes, you may be a Free Spirit in a Competitive milonga, but you might still be able to enjoy yourself.

For the first three visits, your mind may plays tricks on the way you remember things. A more effective way to know how likely you are to have a good time, is to keep a journal, or at least some scribbled notes. Nothing complicated, just write down where you went, when you got there, what time you left and the number of dances you had that you wanted and you enjoyed. After about three visits, you'll have an idea of how predictable a place is and whether it suits you.

(A lot of people who do Argentine Tango are scientists and engineers – if that's you, or you're good at maths, feel free to draw S curve graphs, work out the standard deviation, etc.)

Something else to consider is the total time spent travelling to and from a venue. Is it worth a three hour round trip for an hour's dancing? What if the dancing is really good? What if sometimes it's great but sometimes it's awful? Likewise, you might be willing to take bigger risks going to a venue that's only ten minutes away than with one that's an hour, or more, away. In larger cities, another option is to go onto other milongas. Yes, it took you an hour to get there, and the first milonga is deserted, but from here, it's only a five minute walk to the next one. Also, be wary of being trapped if someone else is your only way home. I've been to a truly awful milonga that took me four hours to get there. But because it was on a Sunday in the middle of nowhere, I had no choice, but to wait for it to end and my friend to drive me home. (Fortunately, even the middle of nowhere had a Diner, so I spent most of the afternoon there, enjoying their home-cooked food.)

It also helps to have a baseline to compare the experience of going to a milonga with. Any time you're doing tango, you're giving up the opportunity to do something else. Now that might be staying at home in front of the tv, but it might also be going out with non-tango friends, or spending time with your family. Or you might actually like watching TV, knitting, reading and so forth.

If instead of going dancing you'd stayed at home with a dvd and a pizza, in hindsight, would that have better? If on the other hand, you're "escaping" the children for the evening, you might have a considerably lower standard for "better". (Though in that case, the cinema might have been a better bet...) Or if you're Competitive, you may well be willing to accept the mantra of "no pain, no gain." There isn't a "right" answer to any of this, other than what you decide it is.

If you don't go to a milonga, no matter how wonderful people tell you it was, you don't really know if you'd have had a good time there or not. Fear of Missing Out, motivates a lot of people, to the extent it's now a popular advertising strategy. "This will be your only opportunity to..." and the implication that Everyone else will be there. This is somewhat true if you're part of a group with a pyramid scheme. Otherwise, relax. There will be other dances and no shortage of people willing to sell you shoes, workshops and so on.

The subject of cognitive bias is huge. You can feel you've been sitting out FOREVER, when it's only been five minutes. (Ok, yes, I realize to some of you that is forever, please never be in the same car as me on a long journey. "Are we there yet?" loses its charm after the tenth repetition...) You can use the guideline of "five tandas per hour" to reality check if you feel you're not getting any dances. Bear in mind, two consecutive tandas spent not dancing, is getting on for half an hour, but if they're the only two you don't dance in two hours, then you may feel you're doing well. Again, you get to set the standards however you want to.

Another thing to consider, is how resilient are you to variation? If you turn up to the same venue for three weeks and for two of those weeks, you get all the dances you want, but on the third, you end up sitting out for most of the night, is that going to work for you if that pattern continues in the future? One solution to variation is that by going to several venues, statistically, you get less variation overall. So for example, you may know that going to three venues will mean you receive nine or ten dances over the week, but you'll have no idea how many you're going to get at each venue on any given night.

The Magic Number

There's a magic number of people in a milonga who want to dance with you pretty much regardless (though annoyingly, this number can be zero). Who these people are specifically, can change from night to night and can even change at different times during the milonga, but we'll get to that in a bit.

There's also a magic number of people who won't dance with you pretty much regardless (fortunately, this number can also be zero).

Let's take a milonga, that has a hundred people.

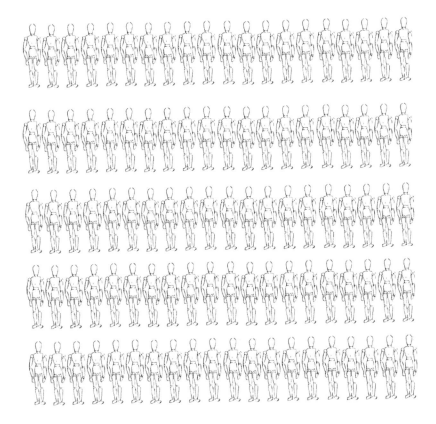

This milonga lasts four hours, assuming the class doesn't over-run, the DJ starts on time, no-one does a performance... There's usually about five tandas every hour (don't worry, the maths won't get complicated!) That means there's about twenty tandas available throughout the night. So even if you turn up at the very beginning, you simply don't have enough time available to be able to dance with everyone there.

If you only want to have one tanda with each person, then you just need the magic number of people who want to accept your invitation to be at least twenty. It doesn't matter how many don't want to dance with you. You can literally be in a room with eighty dancers that can't stand you, but twenty who adore you and you can happily dance every single tanda, all night long, with the people who adore you, one after the other! Like this...

Indeed, for Nurturers and the Competitive, if you're willing to dance multiple tandas, a few, or even, one person may be all you need. It's also worth considering how much effort you want to spend getting invitations. Taking a fixed partner with you, or joining a group might be a better solution for you. Or part of a better solution.

Lowering the Magic Number

Let's look at what can lower the number of tandas you're going to dance and so the number of people you'll need.

You might arrive later and/or leave early.

Dancing for four hours straight is pretty exhausting, so you might want to sit out a few.

The DJ might play some music you just *hatehatehate*.

There might be a performance, or a novelty tanda, such as salsa.

It also scales down for venues which are much smaller. Consider a venue that only runs for two hours. At five tandas an hour, that's now only ten tandas in total for the entire evening.

The logistics of getting partners can vary significantly between venues. Some places are more difficult than others, often due to their layout and lighting. Likewise, no-one uses dance cards, so sometimes you're just out of sync with the people you like and you're not free at the same time.

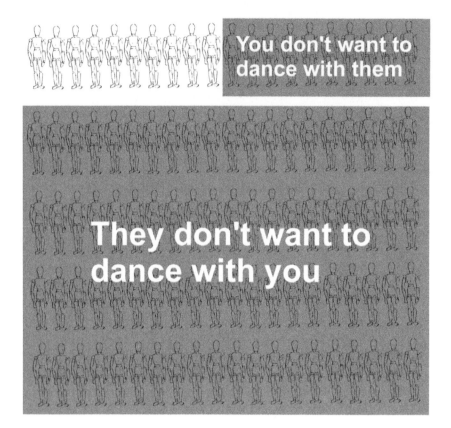

And of course, just because someone wants to dance with you tonight, doesn't mean you feel the same way. You'll want to factor that in too.

Predicting the future

The next thing to consider is how "stable" the milonga is. Various things can affect who turns up, include a visiting superstar DJ or teachers, competing venues and Events on the same night (or them being closed on a given evening), visiting contingents from other countries, live music, student exhibitions and so on. Which means a venue can vary from this

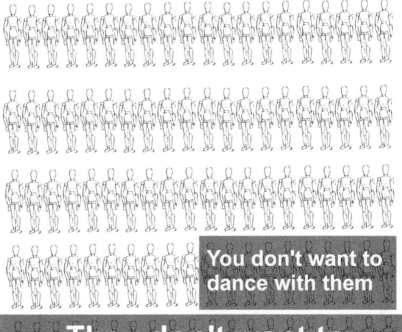

You don't want to dance with them

They don't want to dance with you

to this

You don't want to dance with them

They don't want to dance with you

Fortunately, you can find out if a lot of these effects are happening ahead of time, by looking on social media.

How to cope when (almost) no-one wants to dance with you

Let's take another look at the last one, because it represents a big problem. I've actually been in this situation. I found the magic one person (who I'd never met before), danced for an hour with her and then went home. The trick was finding her without going through the soul-destroying process of being turned down by sixty others first! Now let's look at a less extreme problem. This is still a pretty hostile milonga, but...

Whether this is a good or a bad milonga, really depends on what you know. If you don't know how to spot the partners you want to dance with, who in turn want to dance with you, then, it's horrifying. There's a lot of dancers there who are going to turn you down. You *can* use statistics - realistically if you ask three people, then most of the time, one of them will say yes. But you need a certain personality to be able to keep doing that all night. (Although if that's you, and you want to, then by all means go for it!) A common experience is to look around in a milonga like this one and feel increasingly overwhelmed with uncertainty. After asking and being turned down a few times, it doesn't take that much to feel totally disheartened and give up. Which is a shame, as the next person would often have said "Yes."

But if you look again, you only need twenty people to dance every single tanda for four hours straight and the above has **thirty**! It should be a blissful venue where you're spoilt for choice all night. Which is worth remembering next time you're looking around and getting little to no interest, or you've had several "No"s.

It's also worth bearing in mind that you're unlikely to ever get information this accurate and specific as to how many people do and don't want to dance with you. A lot of it's going to be based on assumptions, which are going to vary in their accuracy. What it does is help you be realistic about what you actually need. It also helps you get a feel for how easy it was at a specific venue and how repeatable it is.

Chapter 4 - Figuring out who wants to dance with you

"My goal now is to dance all the dances as long as I can, and
then to sit down contented after the last elegant tango some
sweet night and pass on because there wasn't another dance left
in me."

~ Robert Fulghum

The fundamental mistake most people make when it comes to trying to invite others to dance is that they're focused on the wrong part of the problem. Like the owner of the car with the empty tank from Chapter 1, they're worried about how smoothly they can change gears, when they need to be looking for gas.

How to look like you want to dance

The first step in conveying to others that you want to dance, is how you sit and stand. You want to avoid looking like you're at an unpleasant job interview. As a rule of thumb, if you're a man, sitting or standing in a more relaxed pose is the way to go. Lean back, rather than slouching forward, or sitting bolt upright. Have your feet apart and your hands somewhere outside your legs, like the figure on the left in the image below. Avoid crossing your arms and legs, or locking your knees, like the figure on the right. Don't fidget or play with your drink or phone. In particular, keep away from holding your drink up in front of you like some kind of shield.

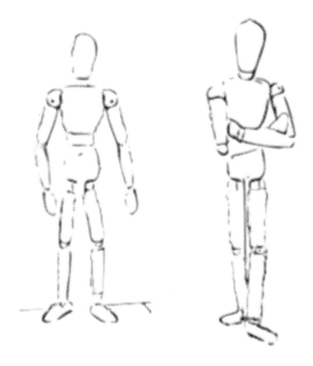

Likewise, for a woman, try to avoid the uncomfortable "job interview" pose of sitting straight on to the dance floor with your legs crossed. Instead, chose one of the front corners of the chair and sit on it, turning yourself so your knees are facing diagonally in the same direction as the corner, rather than directly towards the front. Now tuck your feet back under the seat. It doesn't matter if you cross them or not, though you'll find it's easier getting up to dance if you don't cross them, especially in heels.

Lean forward, almost as if you're bowing and then bring your chest up, so it's pointing horizontally into the room. This in turn will cause you to naturally look ahead to where people are, rather than down at the floor. You want your body to be following the contours of curves, rather than rigid lines. You can also use dissociation to have your upper body facing forward to the dance floor when your body is facing to the side, which has the added benefit of subtly showing that you know what dissociation is (even if you don't!) Turning your upper body and face from the dance floor, towards people you want to invite has a powerful effect.

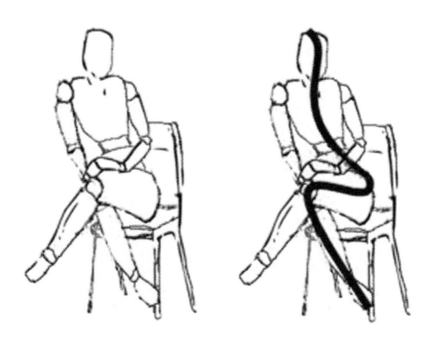

It's also worth considering that there may be times when you want to be left completely in peace. In which case, playing with your phone or hunting around in your bag are effective ways to make yourself look unapproachable. You can also have a "deep conversation" with a friend. This can be made much more effective by taking the time to re-position yourself so that you're looking away from the dance floor, ideally in the direction of a nearby wall. This hinders others from getting into a spot where they can make eye contact with you. It won't stop the truly determined and is generally less effective in a Cooperative venue. On one occasion, I ended up dancing in socks with three women. A friend pounced on me as I'd taken my street shoes off, but hadn't had time to put my dancing shoes on yet. She was promptly followed by two others who didn't even give me a chance to make it back to my seat before grabbing me!

(Hint: if you want to talk to your friend, but still want to make it clear that you're available to dance, do the opposite. Don't position yourself directly facing your friend. Instead, sit or stand slightly side on and facing a direction that you can be easily invited from. Also, use your body language to give the impression that you're just making small talk and would much rather be dancing, rather than looking like you're deep into a discussion on how to solve World Hunger.)

In the process of learning how to shift your body language to convey whether you want to dance or be left alone, you'll also find you can read other people's intentions more clearly. A good rule of thumb, is that people who are doing all the right things to look like they want to dance with you, probably do!

Resting face

A rather sweet idea, suggested by J Michael Strazynski is that

"During the day, we all put on the face we think will do us the most good. But at a certain point in your sleep, as you relax, your true face is revealed."

I don't know if he just thought this was a cool idea, but it turns out that science agrees with him.

Your face has a default setting which it reverts to when you're fast asleep. It's based on the facial expressions you use the most. If you frown and glare and lot, then that's what your resting face will look like. Smile a lot however, and you'll smile in your sleep. But this also happens to a lesser degree, when you're awake and not concentrating on "doing something" with your face.

You know how when someone tells a joke that's not really funny, but to be polite, you force a smile? That's "doing something" with your face. You're putting on the face you think will do you the most good. Next time you're out shopping, look at the faces of people around you. Most people are zoned out and you'll see a lot of "resting faces".

This means a number of important things. Someone looking at you like they're truly fed up, may be completely unaware that's the expression on their face. It may simply be their resting face's default look and have nothing to do with you specifically.

Likewise, it's a good idea to go and stand in front of a mirror, close your eyes and just let your mind drift. Think about the shopping, or the washing up, or pink elephants. It doesn't really matter. Then gently open your eyes. What you're seeing is probably your resting face. You can also just keep your eyes closed and take a quick video clip, or selfie. Bear in mind what this looks like when you're making eye contact with people, especially if your default look is "Why are you bothering me?!"

People-watching in a milonga can also give you useful insights. If someone normally looks grumpy, but their face lights up when they make eye contact with you, that's a Big Clue. If someone is normally a happy, smiling person, they're probably going to be at the kinder end of the spectrum when it comes to accepting, or turning down dances. They may still say, "No", but you'll probably feel like it was a pleasant experience. Someone who looks like they murder kittens in their spare time is probably not someone you want to experience being turned down by.

"Dooooinggg!"

To take the concept a step further, not only do you have a resting face, you also have a resting energy. Ask yourself, who do you know that's a happy ball of sunshine? Who do you know that's always tired? If you have a "grumpy" resting energy, trying to smile can come across as false, or a bit "off." You'll also need to do something to give off happy energy as well. Take a moment and think of something that makes you smile. For one follower, the sound of "Dooooinggg!" brings back a memory that makes her instantly smile. For me, it's the look on Billy's face as he told us his Brilliant Idea. Get that memory in your mind and you'll have a friendly, natural smile, inside as well as out.

However, some find shiny, happy people to be annoying and tiring. They'd much rather be around the kitten murderers. So there's also something to be said for not smiling.

Just be you.

Whether that means glaring, looking bored, tired, or whatever. You'll still attract people who want to dance with you.

Ultimately, it comes down to knowing that you have options. Try them out and see which get you the dances that you want.

Eye contact

At this point, rather than blindly guessing at people to ask, you've taken some time to look around the venue and now you have a feel for who wants to dance with you. Hopefully by watching them, you've also got an idea of what type of dancer they are and what tactics you'll need to make your invitation successful. Whether you're interested in Competitives carefully filtering while huddled in a group, Cooperatives chatting to everyone, Nurturers with a fixed partner, or Free Spirits flitting around.

Human beings are social creatures, so making eye contact by itself isn't a confirmation that someone wants to dance with you right now. It could simply mean they're admiring your clothes, or that they're actually looking at someone else nearby. If you want to be cautious, see if you can make eye contact with them again. The first time could have been random, but it's fairly safe to treat a second, or third, as a deliberate invitation. At that point, they're most likely trying to let you know they're interested in dancing with you.

Soft focus

There's a distinct difference between someone choosing to look away when you make eye contact with them and someone instinctively looking away because they're shy. The first has a much more confident, calm energy to it, while the latter is much more skittish.

To practice soft focus (also known as "peripheral vision") look at your hand, and then relax your gaze. You'll find you can "see" an area around your hand without needing to look directly at it. The detail gets gradually fuzzier as it gets further from your hand, much as if you'd put a "soft focus" filter over a picture.

Now look at a point about three feet behind your hand and slightly off to one side. Relax your gaze until you can see your hand in soft focus.

If you make eye contact with someone who immediately looks away with an energy more akin to a startled deer, look about ten to fifteen feet to one side of them and slowly count to three. Now change your gaze to soft focus. You're interested in what you can see around the fuzzy edges of your vision. Slowly and calmly start to move your gaze back towards them. Hopefully, they'll look at you again, but they'll catch your soft gaze first. This will then let you continue to move your gaze across, until you're making full eye contact with them, without spooking them.

To practice, look around and choose an object. Look over to one side and gradually sweep your gaze back to look at it, seeing it first in the edges of your soft focus and then gradually bringing into sharper detail as you look at it more and more directly.

This is important, because, if instead of looking away, you just keep staring at them, then when they give you a hesitant second glance, you'll probably just startle them again. This isn't really happening on a conscious level. They're not thinking "Ekk! Look away!" Their survival instincts are making them look away and then they're thinking, "Drat, why did I look away?!"

If they look away a second time, you can simply repeat the above process again. At this point, their freeze/flight/fight instinct should have calmed down enough for things to work. If they're still trying to look at you and then looking away when you make eye contact, bear in mind that you're dealing with someone who's very skittish. But also someone who's now made eye contact with you three times in a row. So you might just want to walk over and ask them to dance verbally. If you do this, be very calm, with no sudden movements. Again, think of trying to approach a nervous deer.

The nice thing about this is that if you're not sure whether they want to dance with you or not, when you bring your soft focus back towards them, if they don't want to dance with you, they won't be looking at you. At all. In fact, they'll be very deliberately looking somewhere else. With a little experience, you'll learn how to accurately tell the difference.

Successfully making and holding eye contact by itself, just lets you know that the other person is interested. You don't have to act on it. You can also act on it later. Or you can go and verbally ask them. All we've dealt with so far, are simple effective ways to massively reduce the risk of you being publicly rejected and embarrassed, while focussing your time and energy on your best prospects for dances.

Frankly, during the cortina (cor-TEEN-ah, *the cortina is a short piece of music played between each tanda. A tanda is a usually a set of three or four pieces of music intended for dancing tango. Ideally the cortina is sufficiently different from the music being played for dancing. The floor is usually cleared, except for people wishing to continue dancing together. They can choose to either remain where they are, or stay together and move off to the side, so as not to obstruct others from cabeceoing each other)*, a lot of the energy that goes into trying to make eye contact is wasted effort. It tends to involve staring at someone and hoping they'll look back at you and then wondering when you should give up and try someone else? It's a lot like trying to pick the "right" line at the bank. You'll have more success and find it less stressful, if you go directly to the people who are also interested in you, rather than randomly asking all the people you're interested in.

Worthy of an honorable mention is that while you're seated during a tanda, you can make eye contact (remember to smile!) with people who are dancing while they pass by you. It gives you something to do and basically lets you signal interest at point blank range to a significant number of dancers over the course of a tanda. It's also practically invisible to everyone else in the venue.

What about the people who you want to dance with, who don't make eye contact with you? Does this mean that you won't be able to get a dance with them? Not really, but it does mean that you're going to have to do more work than you would with someone who's already meeting you halfway.

Before we get into this, bear in mind that on the whole, "sociable" women have a good sense of peripheral vision and awareness of their surroundings. If someone looks like a social butterfly, comfortably chatting away like she owns the place, and she "doesn't see you", it's probably because she's politely choosing not to.

Men tend to be less skilled at this, as it's usually not really something they need all that much in daily life. When men give each other "hard looks" they don't tend to be subtle about it. Tango also attracts a lot of people who quite simply aren't social butterflies, and this is where most of the confusion about whether they've seen you or not, comes into play.

People in trances

In their everyday lives, people spend more and more time "zoned-out". It used to be that joggers and teenagers were the only ones who wore earphones in public. Increasingly commuters and even people shopping in grocery stores, use them too. As this becomes increasingly the norm, the number of "space cadets" in milongas also seems to be gradually rising. At any given time throughout the night, there are usually some people sitting and standing around in trance states who might be willing to dance with you.

For many, there's a point during the tanda where they basically give up hope of getting to dance. It's usually about halfway through the first song, unless the milonga is completely chaotic, in which case they may hold out hope a bit longer. After that point, they just zone out. They're not trying to filter or screen, they just don't expect anyone to ask them now that it's gotten this far through a tanda.

Paying attention to their resting face and energy, as well as their type, will give you an idea of how receptive they're likely to be to you "waking them up" and inviting them to dance and the best approach to use.

Making discrete eye contact from across the room isn't going to work in this case. One follower actually tried waving both her arms at me from across the room once when I was "zoned-out", to no avail.

I've seen people stand directly in front of someone and lean over to force eye contact. It worked, and made sense to their Competitive mindset that they'd Done It Properly, because they didn't speak and so hadn't asked verbally. However, it baffled the surrounding people as to why, at that point, they simply didn't just say something?

Going over and saying "Hi" is probably going to make things go a lot smoother when dealing with someone in a trance.

A non-verbal alternative, is to go to within about six feet of them and make a small, relatively quick movement within their line of sight, as that tends to instinctively break people out of trances. By this, I mean step a little faster, or maybe let your hand tap against your leg as you walk. It's definitely not waving your hand in front of their face or jumping up and down. It's not a signal to them directly. You're not trying to get a waiter's attention (actually, please don't don't wave your hand in a waiter's face either.) You just want them to wake up. Like moving the mouse a little when your computer is in Sleep Mode. If it doesn't work, leave them in peace.

Again, you want to calibrate this to the type of person and venue. Cooperatives and Free Spirits are usually going to be more welcoming. Competitives and Nurturers may have actually chosen to zone out as a defense mechanism against being asked. Shiny, happy people will probably react more pleasantly, whereas even if a kitten murderer does decide they want to dance with you, their initial reaction may well be a bit more abrasive.

As I said earlier, there will probably be a brief moment of them being somewhat startled and confused. This is where it's important to smile keep your distance and not make any sudden moves. Their instinctive brain is currently "freezing" and is debating a choice between fight/flight, or engaging social niceties. So give them a moment.

Nodding, offering a hand, or simply saying "Hi, would you like to dance?" can help speed up the process of them figuring out what you're doing, but again, be warned that some Competitive dancers frown on any kind of hand-offering or verbal asking.

This isn't an automatic pass, so be prepared to graciously accept a "No, thank-you" from them.

Chapter 5 - Cabeceo or asking verbally?

"Para bailar con vos hay que secar numero, pero la espera vale la pena (To dance with you I have to line up, but the wait is worth the prize.)"

~ Anon

Although the word "cabeceo" just means "nodding" it's also often used to mean an entire process of invitation, from soft focus gazing, to the making eye contact, to nodding, to walking over, to standing and entering the dance floor. If someone says "they use the cabeceo" they don't mean they just go around nodding in the hope of getting a dance. At least, I hope they don't...

When it comes to getting the dances you want, it doesn't really matter whether the cabeceo is "right" or "wrong", or even which version is "right" or "wrong". Instead, you need to know how, when, where and with whom, the different methods of invitation are going to work best for you.

The way the cabeceo works, is something that people tend to have strong opinions about, but is often a mess in reality. Frankly, in many places, the cabeceo has been mystified to the point of being broken. In particular, so many people, venues and groups have put their own twists on it, that it can feel far more like a secret handshake, than a well-established social more.

To further complicate matters, these variations tend to contradict each other. One group will say the follower has to remain seated, until the leader offers their hand. Another says, the follower should stand when the leader gets to them. Another, that it's the height of bad manners for the leader to offer their hand to the follower, while yet another insists that they do!

As if that wasn't enough, people who swear they only use the cabeceo, will then cheerfully turn to the other members of the group sitting at the same or next table and ask them to dance. However, this tendency can work to your advantage. I've noticed that if someone really wants to dance with you, they'll make exceptions for you regarding their version of the cabeceo. This means it's possible to both bypass it, and in doing so, know that this person really values this opportunity to dance with you.

"So, how does the cabeceo work?"

At its heart, the cabeceo is a way of indicating you want to dance with someone from a distance. The exact minimum distance (like almost everything about the cabeceo) is a point of contention. In some venues, it's simply too dark to cabeceo someone from across the room. The exact mechanics vary wildly, but in general, smiling helps. The basic gist is you look at someone. This is called the "mirada" (mee-RA-da – *looking at someone to invite them to dance)*. If they look back at you (their mirada), give them a moment to maintain eye contact. Then nod (your cabeceo).

Usually the leader then walks towards the follower, especially if the follower is seated, though there's no reason you can't both walk towards each other, or indeed the follower can walk to the leader. Keep looking at each other as you do this.

If the cabeceo doesn't quite seem to be clicking for you yet, it's worth asking a friend to give you some feedback, or film you "doing the cabeceo" at a práctica. You might have resting murder face. Or you may find that by tilting your head a little in a certain direction, or turning your torso to face them, your intention becomes much clearer to read.

Getting from A to B

Something that usually gets left out of advice on the cabeceo is how to physically walk from where you are, to the other person. Similar to the adage of "a bad workman blames his tools", only start to walk once you've got a reasonably clear path that doesn't involve squirming around people. You also want to avoid routes that involve stepping around bags on the floor, tables and so forth.

If the person you've cabeceoed has to look down in order to safely navigate around any obstacles, keep looking at them, so that they can continually re-establish eye contact with you and feel confident that you are still engaged in the cabeceo with them.

To navigate the edge of the dance floor, things work much better if you step in time to the music, rather than just walk at your own pace. Also, even if it's not written in stone, the dancers have right of way. The leaders have more than enough to cope with as it is, without you charging down their blind-side and pushing past them. (If you're a leader, bear in mind when you're dancing that the bar staff and other non-dancers often don't realize this!)

There are different schools on thought on what you should do when they finally arrive. Some followers maintain you should look at them expectantly and wait for them to stand. Some will wait for you to offer them your hand and / or verbally ask. Others feel followers should stand up as the leader arrives. If you're not sure, pay attention to what they do with other dancers. You may well find that there are multiple schools of thought present in the same milonga.

Some dancers feel that it is acceptable, especially in darker venues or ones with numerous obstructions such as pillars, to do a "wandering cabeceo". For this, you try to make eye contact as you walk around the venue. This can be done by both leaders and followers. The main difference is that it can be done at a much closer range, although again, it varies wildly as to exactly how close is considered to be acceptable. Because this tends to happen faster, when doing this you may need to give the other person a moment for their brain to catch up to what's going on. So if they look at you blankly or startled, it isn't necessarily a "No." It's more a "Please wait a moment while I connect you." If you're close enough to say "Hi", it's probably a good idea to do so as it helps smooth the process. Also if someone doesn't seem to understand the cabeceo aspect, and look at your with a confused expression when you're this close, saying "Hi" and then asking them to dance, will gracefully resolve the situation.

"Hey Honey, I'm over here!"

You use the cabeceo in everyday life, whether it's getting the attention of a barman, or when you see your loved ones coming out of customs at the airport, or meeting a colleague getting off a train.

A good starting point is to think of it, simply as a way for friends to signal they want to dance when they're out of speaking range.

One of the main reasons people struggle with it in a milonga, is they're *trying* to do it, rather than just doing it. Much in the same way most experienced drivers would now fail their driving test if they had to re-take it and do it "properly".

It's pretty much the same social tech you use when you're meeting a friend at a station, or if your significant other has wandered off while you're shopping. You catch their eye and nod with a smile. You don't try to do a specific "looking" technique, or nod at a certain angle. You just do it. If anything, it really comes down to that (hopefully pleasant) feeling when you make eye contact with someone you like. You meet each other's gaze and then you acknowledge doing so.

Some dancers feel that Tango is a Serious Business and rather than smile, prefer to look like they're a killer robot from the future, sent to assassinate their intended partner. It still works, because it's blatantly obvious that you are either trying to kill or cabeceo them and the context of being a milonga will suggest it's the latter.

Although it makes sense to ask people how their version works, sometimes, following the instructions won't help, because the explanation that people give doesn't match what they actually do. Diligently trying to follow the instructions in this case, is solving the wrong problem. Your ability to do the cabeceo correctly, often isn't what's stopping you from getting dances with this person. Once again, you first need to put gas in the car.

The embarrassment of saying "No"

Some prefer the "plausible deniability" of not having seen you, rather than having to saying "No" to your face, especially with other people watching. This has an interesting benefit to you too. Imagine every tanda you go up to someone and ask them verbally to dance and they firmly say, "No." How long until you give up? Even the occasional

"No" is slowly soul-destroying for many.

Now imagine that instead, each tanda you try to make eye contact with someone and just can't succeed. It's not as draining and carrying on is less stressful.

A common mistake is not realising that just because someone doesn't want to dance with you right now, doesn't mean they're never going to. With the cabeceo method, if circumstances change in your favor later in the night, then they'll accept your invitation. They may even invite you. That's worth considering if you're someone who says, "If someone says turns down my invitation once, I'll never dance with them again!"

A failure to communicate

Imagine you make eye contact, the other person holds it for a moment and as you're about to nod, they then shake their head. Surely they're evil, right? Actually, it could be they think they're doing you a favor. By being less ambiguous, they've let you know to use your remaining time to focus on other people who you might succeed with (and bear in mind, particularly during a cortina, that window of opportunity is pretty small.)

It also means if you try again later, you know that a nod from them is definitely going mean "yes". So your best bet is to smile, give them a nod that says, "Gotcha, thanks" and then move on. Glaring isn't going to help, remember there's a reason you wanted to dance with them a moment ago. However, I would strongly recommend that you don't shake your head to other people in a milonga, as you can ruffle a lot of feathers.

What about when it's blatantly obvious to the point of being rude? For example, the leader makes eye contact, nods, goes over to the follower and when they get there, the follower shakes their head and says, "No."

The worst option - think that they're a stuck-up hotshot and put them on your list of people never to dance with again!

Better option – relax. The rest of the room saw something different. (Or at least the ones who were paying you any attention. Most people are caught up focussing on what affects them, rather than you, especially during the cortina.) They saw you walk up to someone who shook their head and said, "No" but they don't yet have enough information to make a judgement about it. If you responded with a smile and said something pleasant, like "No problem, hope you have a great night", the people who saw that, will assume you're talking to a friend, or that they gave you a good reason, such as they're having a break or don't like the music. So it didn't reflect badly on you at all.

But more than that, it put you in a good light. You came across as happy, relaxed and confident, all good things.

Unless there's a good explanation such as "I'm exhausted, but please ask me later, because I really want to dance with you!" I'd be inclined not to bother inviting them any more that evening, as your time can probably be better spent with others. But I wouldn't bother keeping a Banned list for future milongas, either.

If you want to show you're available for being cabeceoed (or at least available to certain people), looking around, rather than talking to friends, smiling, tapping your foot, or otherwise moving to the music, are all good ways to signal this.

The Hypercabeceo

Some people have a hyper-awareness of their surroundings. I've walked into a milonga, mid-tanda and stood in the shadows and yet from across the room, mid-song, while dancing with her eyes "closed", a follower saw me, waved and then came straight over to see me as it finished!

In theory, the hypercabeceo should make everything a lot easier. If I know someone is hyper-aware and they appear to have not noticed my cabeceoing them, then I know full well, that they've seen me, it that's a deliberate choice on their part to pretend otherwise. At which point I should look elsewhere.

There's a few ways things glitch. The first is when someone who is hyper-aware, doesn't really grasp that most people aren't. This may lead to a lot of confusion, with them making the above assumption that people are choosing to pretend not to have seen them, when in fact they genuinely haven't noticed them.

The second is rarer. Hyper-awareness often comes from a place of deep trauma. As such, some people will make the conscious decision to "turn it off" in venues where they feel safe. They want to be able to relax and unwind for a bit, becoming the archetypal "space cadet" for the evening. Which means it may be much harder to cabeceo them than everyone else. When someone who's hyper-aware tries to cabeceo them, or vice versa, things tend to get messy.

In my experience, the best solution is to agree to use a verbal invitation. If you're in a venue where this is frowned upon, or will cause problems, one work-around is to go over, say "Hi", chat for a few moments and then discreetly verbally ask them to dance. Or you can sit at the same table and essentially do the same thing. You don't need to sit at the same table for the entire milonga. One, or both, of you can wander off and periodically come back if that suits you.

The joy of fans

Milongas can get remarkably hot, particularly in the summer, and having a fan to cool you down can help. However, with a little imagination, you can also incorporate it into your cabeceo. It's worth having a look around the venue to see if there's any general trends that are being used, but don't confuse these local rules with being commonly understood social mores.

It's mainly a blend of flirting, playfulness and role-playing. The Imperious Contessa calmly fanning herself while leaning back in her seat, or The Impish Coquette playing peekaboo with come hither looks from behind her fan. Find what works best for you, depending on your mood. Some days I simply can't do "serious", no matter how hard I try.

From a practical aspect, some dancers prefer to leave their fan on their table when dancing, while others prefer to put it in their back pocket.

The Beggar's Palm

Holding out your hand to someone as an invitation to dance, is often disparagingly referred to as the "Beggar's palm" (as it resembles the way beggars ask for money). This is actually considered the polite and proper way to ask for dances in many other dance forms, so why does it have such a bad reputation in some circles of Argentine Tango?

It depends a lot on how the venue you're at defines "friendliness". Some feel everyone gets to choose who they ask and who they want to dance with.

The problem with the Beggar's Palm is that if you stand directly in front of someone and hold your hand out, it's quite awkward for them to say, "No" as they're clearly rejecting you. In some venues that can have consequences. People may assume they're a stuck-up hotshot for saying "No", or they may even be expected to sit out this tanda, or at least this dance. Some organizers will even go so far as to put this rule in writing.

"You, get over here, now!"

Tango dancers are still human. They make exceptions for all sorts of weird and wonderful reasons. So yes, that guy did just smirk, point at that woman across the room, then point at the ground in front of him, and yes, she did just run across the dance floor to him with a big smile on her face. That does not mean it's going to work if *you* try it on her, or anyone else for that matter!

Asking verbally

"Would you like to dance?" That's basically it. Smiling is a good idea, as is adding a "Hi" at the beginning. You can hold out one, or both, hands. If you do this, think of it more of meeting someone halfway. The aim isn't to grab the other person. You can also do this pretty subtly. Let your hands rest naturally by your sides with your palms facing behind you. Now just rotate one, or, both of your palms over so it's now facing forwards. You don't need to lift your hand or arm at all.

If you're struggling with asking verbally, especially if you're a woman who feels strange about asking men to dance, try going to Cooperative Prácticas where it's much easier.

"Yes, but..."

A popular way to turn down a verbal invitation by those who use the cabeceo, is to say "I only accept dances through the cabeceo." The less experienced will often use "My teacher taught me to only accept dances through the cabeceo". But it's overkill. "No, thank-you" with a smile is usually all that's needed.

However, sadly, sometimes this happens.

Bill walks over to Sophie and verbally ask her to dance. Sophie says, "No", but then gives a reason such as "I don't really like this music." Rather than smiling, wishing her a good evening and walking away, Bill replies "Yes, but..." and proceeds to explain to Sophie why her reason is wrong, such as "I'm such a good dancer, you'll enjoy it anyway." I've seen this go back and forth for a minute, with the person saying "No", getting more and more frustrated.

Just accept that they don't want to dance with you right now. The rest is politeness. However, if they say, "No" and end it with "But come and find me later" take it at face value and try again later, if you want to.

While it's sometimes possible to bully someone into accepting your invitation through continuous "Yes, but..." you'll make a horrible impression to everyone in the room in the process. Also it's really not a nice thing to do.

Some tango dancers maintain that the cabeceo is a Thing of Evil.

What is somewhat confusing is they usually do so for the same reasons as the people who think that asking verbally is a Thing of Evil. They often forget, or aren't even told, that you are allowed to say, "No" to someone who asks with either method. Many of those who are against verbal asking have been burned by the experience of a "Yes, but..." who wouldn't take "No" for an answer.

However, the "Yes, buts..." are a minority who are abusing the spirit of verbally asking and not representative of the actual concept, much like those who stand directly in front of you, staring intently at your face for what feels like an eternity, aren't representative of the spirit of the cabeceo. Like most things in life, either method works fine as long as everyone is on the same page and plays nice.

Shy beginners

There's one grey area, but it's easy to recognize. This is when you invite a shy, inexperienced dancer and they reply "Oh, no, I'm just a beginner." If you're still happy to dance with them, give them a positive one-line reply. Personally, I find "Me too" with a big smile, works well. We both know I'm lying through my teeth, as they've usually been watching me dance, but it successfully conveys that I understand the situation and won't embarrass them.

They may accept, or their equally inexperienced friend will practically shove them into your arms. In which case dance, but be gentle.

Or they'll decline a second time "Thanks, but I really just came to watch", in which case keep smiling, gracefully wish them a good evening and leave them in peace.

In a Cooperative venue, you also have the option of sitting and talking to them to make them feel welcome and introduce them to others, but check you're not getting "please leave me in peace" vibes as they may be a non-Cooperative beginner.

The spectrum from asking verbally to the cabeceo

Although many debate, rather loudly, whether the cabeceo or verbally asking is the "right" way, quoting everything from women's rights to Hitler in the process, in reality, there's a spectrum between those two positions that a lot of people occupy.

In broad strokes, starting from verbal ask and ending with the cabeceo, these tend to look like:

Version 1. Walk straight over, stand directly in front of them, ask them to dance and hold out your hand. (Think Pride and Prejudice, or Modern Jive.) If they don't accept, smile and politely leave them in peace.

Version 2. Walk straight over, stand directly in front of them and ask them to dance. If they don't accept, smile and politely leave them in peace.

Version 3. Walk straight over to them, stand directly in front of them for a moment and invite them through eye contact. (Hint: smiling is a **really good plan** here, but some people find glaring works too.) If they don't accept, smile and politely leave them in peace.

Version 4. Walk over to within about fifteen feet of them and invite them through eye contact. If they don't accept, smile and politely leave them in peace.

Version 5. Invite someone from across the room. If they don't accept, smile and politely leave them in peace.

A good rule of thumb is to match the other person's level of subtlety. If someone seems to be completely oblivious to your presence, then do the same. Not in a standoffish way. Just the same way you don't try to make eye contact with the tables and chairs.

That's just how we do things here

Different places do things different ways. Some really don't care how you invite people as long as it doesn't involve them having to call the Fire Department. Other venues frown on saying "No", some frown on the cabeceo, and some object to asking verbally, but they're usually remarkably clear about it. It should be on their website, the teacher will usually announce it at the end of the class and anyone who works there, or attends regularly, will be able to tell you. If that's not your cup of tea, you're better off dancing elsewhere.

Before you try to convince someone that they're wrong about the way they chose to invite others, ask yourself, what would it take to convince you that you're the one who's wrong about this? Assume it's going to be at least that hard to convince them. Also ask yourself are you willing to listen to their point of view and potentially have your mind changed, because if not, you'll have a much harder time.

Cabeceo beats Verbal?

While they're both useful in different ways, it's worth noting the one big advantage someone using the cabeceo has over someone asking verbally. It works at range. If you were going to ask someone verbally and you realize that someone else is also going to and will get their first, by switching to the cabeceo, you can "win" this race. Assuming your invitation is successful, what will usually happen is that when the other person arrives and asks, they'll be politely told that they've already accepted a dance with you.

Conversely, if you're standing next to someone you want to dance with, it's a bit strange to walk away and then cabeceo them. It's also counter-productive. If the cortina ended and the music that would perfectly suit dancing them comes on, you've got a pretty small window as it is. Walking across the room and then going through the cabeceo ritual may well mean you miss out. A way around this in venues where the verbal ask if frowned on, is simply to state the elephant in the room . "I'd love to dance this with you, but it just seems odd to go and walk across the room to cabeceo you."

Chapter 6 - Solutions for the shy (also useful for everyone else!)

"El tango te espera (tango waits for you)."

~ Anibal Troilo

Being rejected in public, is one of the most common fears. Indeed, for many, the idea of being told loudly in front of a room full of people, that someone doesn't want to dance with you, is worse than the fear of dying.

Fortunately, there are ways around this. (I give modifications for the increasingly shy, as I go along, so if you find yourself thinking "I can't do that, I'd die!" please keep reading anyway. It saves me having to repeat the concepts later on.)

The Magician's Trick

Magicians can make people appear to share the same experience together, but interpret it very differently from each other afterwards. To accomplish this in a milonga, all you're going to do is move from one point in the venue, to somewhere else.

Before you start to move, have a reason in your head as to why. Maybe you're going to get a drink, freshen up, or even literally just move to a different part of the venue. The important thing is you want the next part of the process to be something you're just doing along the way, and not feel like it's the actual goal.

Just before you begin to walk around, take a moment and get that happy memory of your "Dooooinnng!" moment, (see Chapter 4), in your mind and you'll have a natural, friendly, glowing smile.

Head off towards your destination and while you're on your way, just say "Hi" to anyone you pass who you want to and that it feels *easy* to do so. Briefly make eye contact with them, keep smiling, nod, say, "Hi" and keep walking. Don't force it. You're just you're a friendly person on their way to the bar.

Some people will deliberately avoid making eye contact with you. This isn't a problem. Just leave them in peace and keep going to get your drink, or whatever.

Others will be in a trance, or caught up in doing something else. You might manage to say, "Hi" to someone who was in a trance. In which case, it's not unusual for them to look a bit startled, or confused for a moment, while their brain catches up. Think of it as the equivalent of your PC's mouse arrow turning into an hourglass symbol for a second or two.

If this happens, stay at a comfortable social distance, usually more than five feet, unless the venue is very crowded and keep smiling. These two things communicate on a powerful, and more importantly, quick, level that you're not a threat. It's fine to stay in motion as you're doing this, you don't have to stop. Your priority is getting to your destination. Saying "Hi" along the way is just incidental.

By the time you've got to your chosen location, you now have a good idea of who's open to the idea of dancing with you, who's lost in distraction and who doesn't want to dance with you right now. A hint, the one's who seemed happy and warm towards you are going to be the ones most likely to dance with you.

That was your perspective of what happened. But what about everyone else in the room?

Those who avoided your eye contact and who you left alone, felt you respected their choice. If they feel like dancing with you later in the evening, you haven't burnt that bridge. In fact, you've actually improved your chances.

Those in a trance, who didn't respond, had no clue you were there.

And anyone else in the venue that noticed you, just saw a sociable person going from A to B and saying "Hi" to some people they know along the way.

Wait, when did I say anything about only saying "Hi" to people you know? I didn't. This is the beauty of the Magician's trick. Any people who see you doing this, will simply assume that you know the people you are saying, "Hi" to, because in context that's what is usually means. Much in the same way you usually assume someone wearing a police officer's outfit, is in fact, a police officer.

At this point, even if you weren't able to make eye contact with anyone, no-one is thinking, "What a loser!" because all they saw, if they noticed at all, was someone walk over to the bar, or a different part of the venue. There's zero embarrassment on your part.

Also, you're not restricted to doing this just the once. Think about how often you really do move around a venue during the night.

Hidden opportunities

Another version of this, that particularly suits getting dances with Competitive dancers, is to wait until the person you want to dance with is at a point in the tanda where they're not going to be dancing. About halfway through the first song of a tanda, most people who aren't dancing give up. You can usually see a dramatic shift in their body language. They stop being "perky". And of course, people go to get drinks, or stretch their legs. The timing is important here. By approaching them at this point, you want to give off the vibe of "I'm just a friendly person here to chat", rather than "Please dance with me!" Smile, nod, say, "Hi."

A hint, if they say, "No thanks." or something similar, then you're giving off "Please dance with me!" vibes. Just smile and say, "Oh, I don't want to dance." And then chat. If that sounds like I just told you to sprout wings and fly, then "What do you think of the music tonight?" will usually get you started. But like Cinderella approaching midnight, you want to get out of there before they start to feel social pressure to ask you to dance. At that point, just smile and say "Have a good night. See you later" and wander off. You want to leave on a good impression. Don't wait for things to get awkward.

If they start giving you "go away" body language, such as crossed arms, a lack of smiles, continually looking past you, etc., then definitely take the hint. But, and this is important, as you leave them in peace, you still smile and say, "Have a good night" like you're saying it to a friend. There is no downside to this. There are, however, several upsides.

Again, you've demonstrated that you respect their boundaries and The Way Things Should Be Done. If someone's good enough for you to be making this effort to get a dance with them, they've probably had people do this before who wouldn't take the hint. You've just demonstrated that you're not one of those people and that it's safe for them to talk to you again in the future.

You want to create a positive, safe impression in their heads, so they know you won't desperately hang around them, until they either tell you to go away, or begrudgingly ask you to dance to get this over with. Establish yourself as Mr or Ms Sociable. After you've done this, you'll probably be able to return to them later on during the night and talk some more. When you do this, you'll also notice a big increase in interest from some of those that you've already talked to.

Getting their first name (and remembering it!) is often effective, as people will tend to treat you in a much friendlier way. This technique is best used in smaller places, early on in the evening. That way, as the night progresses and everyone naturally starts to relax and open up more, your options will continue to increase. Plus, you won't have the problem of trying to make your first impressions when it gets louder, more crowded and potentially more competitive.

The Magician's dual reality trick also kicks in. Those tweaks mean instead of the situation where the other dancers watched as you approached a stranger, asked for a dance and were rejected, what they think they saw, was that you went over to someone you know, but they were in a bit of a grumpy mood. You chatted with them for a bit and then wished them a good night.

A version for those who find the idea of saying "Hi" daunting, is simply to walk past at the speed you would as if you were going to say, "Hi" and see how they react, i.e. for this version you're not going to say, "Hi." Some people will still make eye contact and smile back. Indeed, some will say "Hi" to you first.

Where did they put my cereal this week?

Another approach which has no risk whatsoever, is looking around the room in the way you look down the grocery store aisles when you're trying to figure out where they've moved your favorite breakfast cereal to? Only instead of cereal, you're searching for eye contact. Again, there will be people who are in a trance or distracted. There are also people who are actively avoiding making eye contact. These aren't the first choice for the people you're going to try to get dances from. Yes, you can get them to become interested in you, but why do the extra work when there are easier options? Why swim across a river, when there's already a bridge you can simply walk across?

Do this a few times and you'll find the people who really want to dance with you. You'll know when you find them, because they'll be glancing back at you and the area immediately around you. And again, people can warm up to you over the course of the milonga. Some people will want to see you dance with someone else first. Others have to dance with certain people in a specific order before they can get to you. Perhaps they want to dance with you to a certain orchestra, or they might hate dancing milonga and they know that's the upcoming tanda. They may even want to warm up with other people first, so they can really enjoy dancing with you! "Not interested" actually means "not interested at the moment."

If you're inexperienced or shy, it's often a natural reaction to look away when someone makes eye contact with. It will get easier with experience, so don't beat yourself up over it. You might want to consider trying out some Cooperative venues as they're a much gentler way to ease yourself into this process.

Soft focus

If you're too shy even for that, well first of all, have a hug. Secondly, well done on summoning up the courage to go to a milonga.

You're now going to combine soft focus (from Chapter 4) with "searching for your cereal". Rather than looking directly at someone and making eye contact, you're going to focus at a point somewhere around, or behind them, so you can see them in soft focus. At this stage. you're not going to look at them directly. You're just paying attention to who's glancing over at you repeatedly. They're the ones who are most likely to want dance with you.

Even Wallflowers get to dance

And for the ultimate in shyness, just sit there and smile, without looking at anyone. There's probably at least one person in the room who will come over to you and ask you to dance. I would strongly recommend attending a Cooperative venue if you want to use this route.

I remember dancing with a Cooperative woman, at a Competitive venue, who remarked that she'd seen that a man hadn't danced all evening. Apparently he'd asked one woman and been told "No" rather bluntly. This had put him off risking asking anyone else to dance. My partner was going to ask him after we finished our tanda. She was a lovely follower, and it would have made his evening. Unfortunately, as there were only two tandas left, he decided that tonight just wasn't his night and got up and went home. If he'd just stayed put for one more song...

Friends with benefits

You can also take friends along with you, or indeed, let friends take you along with them. All the social mores about working out who to dance with and when and how and so forth, pretty much dissipate with your friends, especially if you're sitting next to them. You might still make eye contact with a friend who's across the room, as it's easier than shouting at them.

In this case, any "No"s are definitely not a rejection of you and are about other factors entirely, such as "I hate this music", "Some idiot just stomped on my foot", "I really need to rest", or "I'm think I'm about to get a dance with someone I've been pining over for months!" Likewise, you can go and chat to friends at any time, just be aware that in doing so, you may be deterring people from asking both of you to dance, as they don't want to disturb you.

Talking to people

Although it's quite possible to spend an entire evening at a milonga without saying a word, at some point, you'll probably want to talk with someone, especially if you're visiting a Cooperative milonga. Perhaps between songs, or if you've asked them to dance early in the cortina, or when the DJ's messed up and there's a rather long pause as the music suddenly dies and silence descends.

At this point, the idea of suddenly coming up with scintillating conversation with a complete stranger is probably terrifying. Fortunately, 95% of tango conversations are the same. So much so, that you can use the following with everyone you meet throughout the night. You can also recycle them and use them at the next milonga you go to, and with the same people as the night before.

Sometimes, you'll be chatting with someone who isn't good at conversation. Possibly they're also shy, maybe they got rather zenned out while dancing and are taking a moment to re-engage the "talking" part of their brain. Fortunately, Tango has a different set of social mores when it comes to small talk, than, say a dinner party. The following contain a mixture of statements and questions. This prevents you falling into the increasingly awkward situation of feeling like it's some kind of weird job interview where you ask them a list of questions and they give you one word answers. You can have a thirty second conversation, using just this and consisting of nothing more than one word answers and "Uh huhs" from them and, surprisingly, rather than praying for the earth to swallow up at least one of you, actually, it'll be fine.

You can also use these for "normal" conversation. Tango is a social event after all. They're a good way to ease into talking, especially if you've just spent the day only sending electronic messages to your co-workers who sit 3 feet away from you, so you don't have to talk to them and then promptly put your earphones in and stared at your tablet for the journey home.

At this point, it's tempting to start worrying about finding some kind of "magic bullet". The conversation piece that will suddenly open them up and make everything work wonderfully. In reality, people who click with you, will do so. These sentences provide the other person with plenty of opportunities to expand and indeed jump off into other topics they're enthusiastic about. If after about a minute, they're still just giving you one word answers, it's probably best to accept that right now, that's the headspace they're in and it's unlikely to change.

You use these in any order.

Introduce yourself

"Hi, I'm Oliver." If they don't offer their name, ask them. When they give it, repeat it, to show you heard them properly. This may also help you remember them next time.

"Hi, I'm Oliver" **pause** *"And you are?"*

"Chloe."

"Chloe. Pleased to meet you."

If you've met them before, great them by name

"Hi, Sophie"

or *"Hi Sophie, haven't seen you in a while"* if you haven't seen them in a while.

If you can't remember their name, just say so

"I'm sorry, I've forgotten your name?"

When they tell you, it's a kindness to then offer your name, and let them act like they remembered it anyway.

"I'm sorry, I've forgotten your name?"

"It's Steve."

"Of course. I'm Oliver."

Other popular sentences include

"I'm trying out new shoes / skirt / top etc"

"Where are you from?" both geographically eg New York, or nationality eg French

"How long have you been dancing?"

"Where did you learn / who taught you?"

"Have you been to – a Festival, Paris, BsAs... - ?"

"I've been to BsAs"

"Are you going to / were you at -Event- ?"

"How's your week been?" - you can ask this on Monday, though *"How has your day been?"* makes a bit more sense. People will often treat this as meaning the week since this milonga was last held.

If you enjoyed dancing with them

"You're really easy to lead / follow"

"You're a really good leader / follower"

"You really feel the music"

"We were great!"

"Mmmmm"

Asking which about the track that was just played will always work, even in venues where the DJ has a sign up saying what is currently playing. It doesn't matter if your partner doesn't know.

"What song / orchestra was that?"

"I don't know"

"Me neither"

However, if they do, then this is a good way to follow on the conversation

"What song / orchestra was that?"

"Di Sarli"

"Really, how do you know?"

Another question that you can ask even if you were in the class is

"Did you do the lesson?"

If the music moved you, or you like what's coming next

"I love vals / Di Sarli / nuevo..."

If you have previous dance experience, so can recognize it in your partner, though be aware that some tango dancers look down on ballroom tango.

"I've done – ballroom / salsa / ballet -. Have you done any other - dances / ballroom / ballet / etc -?"

If they admit to having done ballroom, but seem a bit wary, you can usually compliment them on their floorcraft

"I've done some ballet. Have you done any ballroom?"

"Yes, how can you tell?"

"The way you pay attention to what's going on around you. It's very specific to ballroom dancers"

When it's hot and everyone's dripping with sweat or "glowing"

"I'm hot!"

When the tanda ends

"Is this the cortina?"

When you've lost count of how far through the tanda you've got.

"Was that 3 or 4 dances?"

Or you're not sure how the DJ does tandas, if at all.

"Does this DJ do tandas in threes or fours?"

Cheat sheet

You can take a small piece of paper with you with a few of these either written or printed on it. Have it small enough to fit in your pocket or handbag. Then just try them out throughout the evening. You'll find a number of things happen.

There's a variety of ways for people to respond. Some will pause and think, some may look surprized, some reply and then launch onto a monologue of their own and so on. But with experience, you'll quickly start to see the same reactions occurring over and over. At which point, you'll start to become increasingly confident. You're no longer having to come up with unique witty banter worthy of a sitcom (soooo much easier when you have a staff of trained writers writing the script for you.)

You can also recycle the replies you get.

So with Sally first conversation goes

You - *"Where else do you dance?"*

Sally - *"La Cortina. And you?"*

You - *"Santa Maria"*

Then the next conversation has Marc, asking you

Marc - *"Where else do you dance?"*

You - *"Santa Maria. And you?"*

Marc - *"La Cortina. What do you like about Santa Maria?"*

You - *"Um, well, it's nice. What do you like about La Cortina?"*

Marc - *"It's a really friendly place with a good energy, you know. I always feel uplifted when I'm there and the DJ is great!"*

So now with Beth, you blend that in

You - *"Where else do you dance?"*

Beth - *"Santa Maria, and you?"*

You - *"La Cortina. It's a really friendly place with a good energy, you know. I always feel uplifted when I'm there and the DJ is great! What do you like about Santa Maria?"*

And so on.

Now before you start panicking about having to remember huge scripts and sounding artificial in the process, humans are innately social creatures. We do this instinctively, so you don't need to memorize massive amounts of conversations. By having the same basic conversations over and over, you'll start to subconsciously pick up others' solutions and you'll find they help your own small talk flow better. Being aware of this just means you tend to get better a bit faster.

Also, bear in mind that over background noise and differing accents, sometimes people mishear you. I asked one follower "Where else do you dance?" and she replied "I used to be a ballerina." I assume she thought I said "What else do you dance?"

Chapter 7 - Other approaches to getting dances

"Hold me, feel the music, and give me your soul. Then I can give you

mine."

~ Sallycat

Whether you use a version of the cabeceo, or verbally asking people, this is just one piece of the bigger puzzle. There are other factors and approaches that will let you adjust the experience of each milonga to something that suits you even better. You may find that different methods appeal to you at different venues, or indeed that your preferences slowly change over time.

Social butterfly or mysterious stranger?

An important question for many is how much control you want over who you dance with. If you want to be in the midst of it and favor the role of the social butterfly, make eye contact, smile and say, "Hi" to everyone! You can also introduce people to each other. You'll get more introductions, but these aren't necessarily the ones you want. This can result in you spending a considerable amount of the evening talking. It's also a good idea to do some prep work ahead of time, by posting on the relevant social media Event Page about how you're visiting and looking forward to it. Then tag yourself in the photos afterwards and say how lovely everyone was.

Conversely, the Mysterious Stranger route, of not talking to anyone, except to ask specific people to dance (and with the cabeceo, you can spend an entire night dancing without having to say a word to anyone) will definitely give you much more control over who you dance with. Your big problem is getting a dance in the first place! But if you don't like talking to strange people and want to filter dances, it's very effective.

Being a DJ, Teacher, Demo, Organizer, Professional, Back from Buenos Aires, Shoe Seller, Argentinian, Blogger, had private lessons with a Superstar...

If you fall into one of these categories, less experienced dancers will generally assume you're good (or at least want to see *how* good). If you dance tango seriously for any length of time, you'll find you have an increasing number of these opportunities open to you. The thing no-one points out, is that no matter who you are, beginner or Superstar DJ blogger from Buenos Aires, some people will think you're great, some people who think you're ok and there will be some people who wouldn't dance with you if you paid them.

In theory, the one benefit you gain from having a "Tango Job Description" is that some people are more willing to dance with you in the first place. They're often curious to see if your dancing has changed after you've come back from Buenos Aires, started teaching, DJing, had private lessons and so on. Or they want to know how well the Blogger actually dances. Others will be intimidated and nervously avoid you. You also start to get a reputation, meaning that you'll find it easier or harder to dance with some people, depending on what they're friends have said about you.

However, when it comes to getting dances with each other those who also have Tango job titles, it gets a little more complicated. The longer you do tango, the more likely you are to end doing at least one of the above at some point. There tends to be increasing synergies between the various roles over time. A bit like mushrooms, they all interconnect and support each other below the surface. The workshops or Events benefit from the publicity generated by the Bloggers, making them bigger, better and in turn, able to afford bigger and better DJs and Superstars. Shoe sellers benefit from being seen with their wares at such Events while also acting as a selling point.

The elderly Argentinian may be a Rock Star in the milonga, adored by woman and admired by men, but not so much in their daily life in the Real World. The Bloggers, want to encourage decent events that they can go to, where they in turn buy shoes and so on.

Unfortunately having a Job Title doesn't automatically make you a good dancer. Inevitably, the different temperaments still arise and some will find reasons not to dance with each other. They're just usually more polite about it. No-one will openly turn anyone down and there may be a few dances here and there for politeness sake or to maintain appearances. But if you see two people with Job Titles regularly dancing together and looking like they're enjoying themselves, most likely it's because they actually are enjoying themselves and has nothing to do with the titles involved.

Teachers don't automatically get dances either, but they do usually get grace to "work a room." While Competitive dancers often place a premium on dancing with them, (or at least with the "right" teachers) it's usually not dancing in the social sense. Under those circumstances, teachers are often conscious of how they appear and its effect on their reputation. Even when they're dancing with other teachers or their teaching partner, most find it hard to relax in the scrutiny of a Competitive venue.

How to cope when the milonga is sabotaging you

Sometimes you'll find that your invitations just aren't working. Maybe the energy of the milonga is a bit off, maybe the DJ's playing music that no-one wants to dance to. For whatever reason, you're having a hard time getting a "Yes." Or at least it can seem like a hard time. In reality, you're probably still getting one yes for every three people you invite. A solution is to change the energy of how you ask.

To do this, imagine you're in a milonga with some friends, but the music is dull, the floorcraft is a mess and there's no-one else that you particularly want to dance with. The only upside is that you've haven't seen these friends in a while, and you're enjoying chatting to them.

Time passes and as the cortina ends, you hear a piece of music, that while not great, isn't quite as awful as everything that's gone before and you realize you've been sitting talking for about an hour. So, you say to your friend "Do you want to dance to this?" Your energy conveys that it's a real question, but you're not heavily invested in the outcome. You might even shrug as you ask. If they say they'd rather keep talking and wait for something better, you're fine with that. It's not unusual for people to reply "This isn't too bad. I guess we should dance, given that we are at a milonga" or to wince and say "I'm not really feeling it. So you were saying about..."

That's the kind of laid-back energy you want to use, regardless of whether you're making verbal or non-verbal invitations. You don't necessarily have to shrug, but you can take or leave it. Even if five people in a row say, "No", with this attitude, you don't take it personally, which will let you keep going, until you find someone who is willing to dance despite the current circumstances of the milonga.

The Dark Arts

Sooner or later you'll encounter someone approaching you using stalking, ambushing, pouncing, or acting like they know you.

It's important to first distinguish both the kind of venue are you in and what kind of person is doing the "approaching". Cooperative venues and types, usually favor the ethos of talking and dancing to everyone, so as long as no-one feels they're being greedy and having more than their fair share, everything's copacetic.

However, under those circumstances, these strategies are overkill. It's a lot easier just to wait until the person you want to dance with is available and go and ask them. Even if they're in demand and another person invites them at the same time, they'll usually agree to dancing the tanda after this one with you.

These strategies aren't effective on Free Spirits as they simply don't feel bound by the social mores that make them work.

They can however, really annoy Nurturers and Competitive dancers, both the ones being approached and the ones who see these approaches being used. If you're a Competitive or Nurturer, it helps to be able to recognize them quickly and know how to protect yourself, if necessary. If you wait until it happens to you in a milonga and then try to solve it in under a second, you won't come up with anywhere near as good options as you will by taking a half an hour now. Sit down with a glass of something as you read through this section and think through the various possible scenarios, to help you decide where you want to draw the lines should this happen to you.

Before we get into the specifics, there are basically two lines that people will cross that cause problems. One is getting dances by "cheating" the unwritten Rules of the venue, or that group. The other is trying to pressure someone into dancing, who, given a free choice, wouldn't. It's important to take into account how the person being asked feels about it and how they're reacting. Those who consistently cross these lines, may find themselves persona non grata with a lot of dancers.

The Dark Arts tend to be used in two situations. Either someone wants to get a dance with a specific person and for whatever reason it isn't happening fast enough (or at all!) Or, there's a significant difference between the number of leaders and followers, and someone has had enough of sitting out endlessly because of this number imbalance and wants to dance!

Pouncing or just being pro-active?

There's usually a certain rhythm to the way people ask for dances. I tend to wait until the cortina has ended and the tango music has started to play, before I start asking people to dance. This means that if you ask me before this point, you skip the line. You're also more likely to catch me unaware, as I'm not really in the head-space for invitations during the cortina, which in turn, gives you better odds of success. Or at least it did, until it happened enough that I got used to it.

The problem is that this can easily turn into all-out escalation. Let's say, if nothing had happened, I would have waited for the cortina to end, heard the beginning of a Di Sarli tanda and cabeceoed Agatha.

But instead, Betty pounced on me during the cortina, while Agatha was waiting patiently for the music to start. So Betty got the next tanda instead of Agatha. During the next cortina, Agatha again continued to wait until the end. Only this time Cathy asked me and she did so even earlier in the cortina than Betty. So again, Agatha lost out.

This continues for the next two hours and gets to the point, that as I'm literally leaving the dance floor as a tanda ends, Nicola pats me on the arm and asks me to dance. There's going to come a point where Agatha either gives up, or escalates herself and cabeceos me while I'm still dancing with Nicola!

In fairness, none of the ladies in this scenario have done anything wrong per se. Very few venues have any kind of written requirement for you to wait until a certain point in the cortina before you start inviting potential partners. Those who like to know what the first song is, will get increasingly annoyed as it becomes apparent that if they want dances, they will have to chose "blindly", as all the partners they want are being taken during the cortina. They may attempt to mitigate this by saying "Let's wait and see what it is", requiring you to wait with them until the end of the tanda. But you've still effectively reserved them at that point, although if they don't like the music and won't dance, you're now going to be in the position of having much less people to chose from.

It's also possible to do the reverse of this. Go up to someone early on in the cortina and ask "Shall we see what the next one is?" If they accept, you've effectively reserved them. However, with this version, you retain the option not to dance if you don't like the music that comes on. This works particularly well if both of you prefer to make hear the music before deciding, but are being forced to ask earlier in the cortina by the actions of everyone else.

Number imbalances

When there are far more dancers of one role than the other, it can end up with everyone in whichever role has more people, being forced to either take part in this increasing escalation of asking earlier in the cortina, or risk sitting out significantly more. It's a bit like musical chairs, or deciding just how early you want to leave in the morning to avoid rush hour. If it gets to the point where people are trying to arrange dances during the preceding tanda and then leap on prospective partners as the music is ending, things have got rather out of hand. I've seen dancers thank each other as the tanda ended and then immediately turn and ask the nearest person to dance, without even leaving the dance floor.

At a Competitive or Cooperative Venue, if it becomes apparent that people are "stealing" dances by breaking the rules, the atmosphere is going to get increasingly tense, often bordering on outright hostility.

Here's the thing a lot of people don't realize. Yes, you can use this method to get more dances for that night. But you can put a lot of people's noses out of joint and some of them have long memories. The way you acted tonight, might end up costing you an introduction to better dancers, later down the line.

Competitive groups can mitigate the effect of a number imbalance, by simply dancing within their own group. When travelling to a Competitive venue without their group, the problem they have to solve, is to make everyone else aware of how good they are. This in turn, leads to the dilemma of getting the first dance. You want someone good enough to make you look great, but how do you get a dance with them without them having seen you dancing first? This is where having a job title comes into play to help entice good dancers to invite you. This can be obvious, eg everyone can see you're the DJ, more subtle, such as sitting at the teachers' table, or even dropping into conversation that yes, you're **that** Blogger.

That first good dance can have a domino effect among the other Competitive dancers and get you further invitations. This can be an effective way to get a temporary membership to the various groups present giving you access to their dancers. At the end of the tanda, walk them back to their seat, mention that you're here alone, and say "Hi" to their friends. If they're impressed with your dancing, they may well do the introducing for you.

The mistake Competitive dancers tend to make when they go to other types of venues on their own, is to assume that just being a good dancer will get you invitations, even if there's a number imbalance. However, relying on the tango meritocracy in other types of venue rarely works, because they each approach the problem differently.

Nurturers can simply remain in their small groups. A leader will dance with one follower while two more either dance together, or chat. Then the leader will dance with the next follower and just keep cycling through the three of them all evening. Or vice versa if there are too many leaders. Or indeed a Nurturing couple may simply dance with each other for most of the evening.

Free Spirits are quite capable of amusing themselves with disparate numbers, be it swapping partners mid-dance, having threesomes (or more!) and cheerfully chatting to people. At Cooperative venues, people will share. Women will lead, or Men will follow as required, in an attempt to mitigate matters. And again, chatting will ensue.

Stalking and Ambushing, or just being sociable?

Ok, but what if you want that one Special Person? People are fairly predictable, especially if you've been to the same milonga as them. You can simply wait until they go to get a drink, and then you go and get one as well. Now you can chat to them while they're in the line. Or you can wait until they're standing off to the side, or sitting alone, and then go over and talk to them. At this stage, there's nothing really wrong with this. Even in Competitive venues, Tango is a social event. Over the course of the evening, dancers will often be quite content to spend some time talking. Although, if you're getting "please, leave me alone" signals, then it's polite to do so.

Where it becomes a bit more subjective is when you start talking to them and then ask them to dance, or even skip the talking part altogether. How well they take this, will depend a lot on where they sit on the Cooperative spectrum, how socially pressured they feel and how much they want to dance with you.

Generally speaking, people are less thrilled about being asked to dance when they're taking a breather or getting a drink. Likewise, some will feel that you're putting them in an awkward position by asking them outright. Even if they're sitting in their "spot" they may still feel trapped.

"It's so good to see you again!"

All of these can be significantly enhanced when someone pretends they know you. Because tango tends to have quite a flow-through of people, especially beginners, remembering everyone you've ever met soon becomes increasingly difficult, the longer you've been dancing. People will tend to err on the side of politeness and just go along with it.

The graceful logoff

So how do you defend yourself against these Dark Arts? If someone asks you to dance and you feel awkward about saying "No", then instead you can use "Maybe, later?" or "My teacher told me only accept dances through the cabeceo." You can soften things considerably by then using the graceful logoff. Resist the temptation to give a further explanation. Just say, "Well, you have a good night" and then politely walk away. They'll usually reply "Uh, thanks, you too."

"Would you like to dance?"

"Maybe, later? Well, you have a good night."

"Uh, thanks, you too."

When it's someone who keeps talking to you and it's clear that they will continue to do so, until you ask them to dance, you can also end this situation at any time by using the graceful logoff. Simply reply with a one word answer followed by "Well, you have a good night" and then politely walk away. Again, they'll usually reply "Uh, thanks, you too"

"Good music isn't it?"

"Yes. Well, you have a good night."

"Uh, thanks, you too"

If the conversation has died down to an awkward silence and they're still refusing to leave, rather than giving in and dancing a tanda you don't want to, just make a short one sentence observation and immediately add "Well, you have a good night." Don't give them time to reply and again, politely walk away.

Uncomfortable silence

"It's crowded in here, well, you have a good night."

"Uh, thanks, you too"

Sometimes, you'll never see them again. Which is a big factor when there's a lot of visitors, such as at a Festival or other Event. They know they don't necessarily have to play nice if they don't expect to go back, or if it'll be a year or more until they return, by which time there will be different people there anyway.

Obviously if they've wowed you with their personality, or you've been dying to get a dance with them, then feel free to either accept their invitation or ask *them* to dance.

There have also been times when I've started talking to someone with no intention of asking them and they've asked me to dance. If you're in that confusing area where someone has come up and started talking to you and you're not quite sure if they're just being sociable and you don't know how they'll react if you ask them to dance, assume that after about thirty seconds, "Would you like to dance to this?" is a reasonable question. If they say "no", just nod as if you'd asked them if it's raining outside and then carry on talking as before.

You may find when you're in a conversation, that people come up to either of you. Sometimes to join in, sometimes, just to say "Hi", maybe give you a hug and continue on, or to ask one of you to dance. The reasons for this vary widely. They may be good friends. They may be complete strangers who feel that it's "obvious" you'd rather be dancing than talking, because why else come to a milonga? Unless you're discussing matters of life and death, your friend will almost certainly understand you stopping the conversation with them mid-way, to dance with someone you want to. If you don't want to accept the invitation, just smile, say "Not at the moment, thank-you" and then nod slightly at the person you're talking to. Give the person who asked a moment to gracefully nod back and then carry on with your conversation.

Chapter 8 - Tailoring the milonga experience to you

"Tango came at a time when I very much needed to belong somewhere. Miraculously, tango became where I belonged."

~ Mari J

The venue you where you start is just luck. It's mainly a mixture of proximity to where you work or live and friends you know who go there. I don't know anyone who deliberately travelled to a different country to start learning to tango. This doesn't mean it's a bad venue, but if you're not finding it a good fit, it's probably worth getting out and exploring.

For most people, at any given time, generally roughly a third of venues are awful, a third are ok and third are great. The character of venues change roughly every six months to a year. Most have a shelf life of one to three years. Teachers and regulars change, venues move and close, fashions come and go.

If you're going to give each venue three visits, in a major city, that's potentially a lot of work. On the other hand, if you're finding that your current venue isn't suiting you (or has closed), the odds are in your favor that it'll be better. So while you'd need to visit all the venues to know what your very best options are, you can usually find a new home by trying out two or three milongas, especially if you've taken the time to find the ones that seem to match your type. Although as an added side benefit, trying out new venues will get you noticed. Connections made in one milonga may yield fruit in another.

Now depending on whether you're a glass half full or a glass half empty person, you need to ask yourself "What's the worse time I'm willing to put up with and how often am I willing to put up with it?

What's the best time I want and how often does it need to happen for me to put up with the bad times? How good do I want things to be most of the time?"

So for some people, if they get all the dances they want most evenings, but say, every few months they have a rubbish evening, that might be ok for them. There's no single, correct answer here. You can demand the moon if you want, though the answer may be what you want isn't currently available. Much in the same way if you turn up to a milonga hoping to breakdance, you're going to be probably going to be disappointed, no matter how good you are at getting dances.

Some specific thoughts for when you visit a new milonga.

Who sits where? Does it mean anything?

If a venue has a permanent group, they will usually sit by the DJ, unless this is completely impractical. Chattier people are more likely to spend time by the bar, especially where it's well lit. People who are just there to dance but are open to dancing people, tend to hang around the places where people walk past, e.g. on the way to and from the bar. People who want to carefully choose who they dance with often take position themselves in a corner, often with a group of friends, or in a place where it difficult to walk up to them without it being obvious you want to ask them to dance. But there's no consistent way of telling where the good dancers are, based on where they're sitting.

The one exception to this, is people who are on their own and being ignored. If someone is confident enough to go a new milonga on their own, most of the time they'll have the dancing skills to back it up. If they're visiting from a different town or country, it's even more likely, hence the myth that all foreigners are better dancers than the locals.

The rubbish ones simply don't tend to travel to foreign milongas and hope to be able to hold their own.

There are no Unicorn Glades

A "Unicorn Glade" is a term I coined for the venue that someone will excitedly describe to you as "filled with good dancers" and the "Best venue in the state!" or even the country. Here's the problem, it's rare to have many of the best social dancers at a venue on any given night. What people usually mean, is there's enough people there who they want to dance with and are of a similar type to them, for them to have a good night.

Finding your inner wa

It's possible to adjust how you feel before you even get to the milonga. Psychologists have conducted experiments that show that your stance and posture has a direct effect on how much your body produces certain chemicals, which in turn make you feel happier, more confident and generally able shrug things off. Standing like a superhero for two minutes before you head off to a milonga will boost these chemicals significantly.

Simply stand with your feet slightly more than hip width apart, put your fists on your hips and look slightly up and off into the distance. You can also "top-up" by adopting this stance during the night. For the more shy, there's bound to be somewhere in the milonga, like a stairwell, where you can stand for two minutes undisturbed and unobserved. Just ask yourself, if you wanted to make a phone call in private, where would you go? You can also modify this stance slightly, by simply holding your phone and having a conversation, mainly of "Uh huhs" to it, while standing in this stance. People tend to instinctively ignore people talking on the phone, so as not to appear rude.

Likewise, many find that meditating before setting out, helps to significantly calm your body chemistry, especially if your job is stressful or involves interacting with people in an often unpleasant way, such as working on a Help Desk.

How to avoid feeling tired and stressed

If you consider yourself a "Lark" or a "Night Owl", you'll know that different times of the day suit different people. Some are happy bopping around at 2am, while others rejoice at being awake at 6am. Take a moment to work out which time of the day suits you. Try to chose milongas that match that. For example, you may find that afternoon milongas just feel easier for you, rather than the ones that go on until dawn.

Also, give some thought to resting before you go. At 7pm you may be better of having a nap till 10pm and then heading out to the milonga feeling refreshed, rather than leaving at straight away at 7pm and feeling washed out the whole time you're there. Then again, you might be the sort of person who at 7pm has just enough energy left to get to the milonga, but once you're there is energized by the music, people and dancing. Whereas if you'd sat down on the sofa for "just five minutes" you wouldn't have gotten up again.

The journey to the milonga is another piece of the puzzle. Spending an hour sitting in a car, with the other drivers trying to kill you, is not conducive to inner peace. There was one venue, long since closed, that involved a particularly nightmarish journey for me. However, I discovered a nearby canal that looked like it had popped out of a Beatrix Potter book, complete with friendly ducks. So I took to arriving slightly earlier and after I parked and determined that I was in fact, still alive, I would go to the canal and practice tai chi in front of the ducks, until my serenity was restored.

I've also found, to my surprize, that listening to pop music, or talk radio, makes me notably more aggressive and impatient, whereas travelling in silence, or talking to a real human being, brings out my sense of benevolence and calm. I enjoy classical music on the way home, but strangely, it irritates me on the way there.

Try to come up with at least one, ideally two or more, alternative ways that you could enjoy the evening, should you find yourself sitting out, instead of focussing on "I must get dances!" It might be talking to friends, meeting new people, watching the dancing, people-watching or just drinking wine!

A useful trick, when you've sat out a tanda, is as it ends, walk onto the dance floor and then exit somewhere else as the rest of the dancers begin to clear it for the cortina. It gives you a bit of an energy boost and people assume you've been dancing and so can be warmer towards inviting you. I highly recommend this whenever you've sat out two tandas in a row. It's also possible to invite people while you're on the dance floor.

If you find you're struggling to get dances, take some time to assess what does everyone else here does during the cortina. Do people start pouncing as soon as the tanda ends, do they wait until about ten seconds before the end of the cortina, or do they wait until the music actually starts to play before deciding on potential partners? Is everyone doing the same thing, or are the people you want to dance with doing something different to the rest of the crowd? Try adapting to this, even for just the next two tandas. This becomes particularly important if the people you want to invite are in demand or if there's a significant number imbalance.

When you're alone and not dancing, it's easy to end up standing there, holding onto your drink like an imaginary shield and feeling weird. Instead, try adopting the mindset that you're waiting for a friend, or that your friend has just gone to get a drink, or to freshen up.

When you've been to a milonga a few times, you can start to make it feel more friendly, by looking at the layout and trying to recognize familiar faces. People are creatures of habit. Staff, the barman, DJ and the person on the door, tend to be in the same place. You can have some casual conversations with them throughout the night. Pay attention to the lighting and foot traffic. If you want to say, "Hi" to a lot of people, a well-lit place at the Bar is a good place to be at. If you find yourself retreating into your head, try moving around the venue for a bit, enjoying the music, without caring what others think. Venues can change over time, so if you haven't been there in a while, you might need to re-acclimatize yourself.

When considering where to stand or sit, pay attention to which spots are "owned", those which aren't claimed at all and those which are communal property (common in venues where there's simply not enough seats for everyone).

If you want to be left in peace to choose your dances, or you just don't like talking to strangers, there's usually a shadowy spot or two, often in the corners. Alternatively, choosing a place where someone coming towards you has no chance for a graceful exit if you turn them down, can also be very effective. When someone is unable to make eye contact as they approach, most will try to style it out by simply walking past and acting as if they were heading to another destination all along. However, there's usually a few places where there simply isn't anywhere to carry on to, forcing them to literally turn around and go back the way they came. By the same token, be cautious about inviting people who have chosen these positions! Some will wait until you've come over to them, before they helpfully tell you "No".

The Beginning

The character of each venue tends to change between three distinct stages throughout the evening. I've imaginatively called them the beginning, middle and end. You don't have to be there for all three. To get the most enjoyment, you want to figure out which "golden time" best suits you.

Although the Beginning technically starts from when the DJ starts playing music, if there's been a class beforehand, there can be a certain amount of random shuffling around while people pay. Classes often over-run, meaning the advertized starting time can vary considerably in its accuracy. Those that did the class, may decide to first dance with each other, significantly reducing the available partners for those who didn't. And there's usually some hesitancy all round about joining an empty, or near-empty, floor.

DJs tend to play "easier" music to get the milonga going and help to fill up the floor. No-one in their right mind is going to start with a tanda by Biagi *(Be-Adg-ee — a pianist who specialized in syncopated tango music and formed his own orchestra)* or a milonga tanda. Or a Biagi milonga tanda.

There are essentially three main types of music that are played, "tango", "vals" and "milonga". Depending on the venue, "nuevo", may also happen. The popular approach at the moment is to play songs in groups of either threes or fours called "tandas". It's assumed that you dance the remainder of the tanda with the same person. Some DJs don't use tandas at all and just play continuous music letting the dancers decide how long to dance with any one person. Some dancers will mentally choose to dance three or four and keep track themselves. Others will choose two if longer nuevo tracks are being played.

Why "Thank-you" is messed up in Tango

Sometimes two people are just not meant to dance together. For whatever reason, you will dance and it just will not work. You can make a decision at this point as to whether you think it might be possible to for things to get better. If you don't, the polite solution is to simply say "Thank-you" at the end of the song and walk away. I'll talk more about this in Chapter 13. For now, what's important is to realize if you have a great dance with someone and you say "Thank-you!", it will usually be interpreted as "That was awful and I don't want to dance with you any more." This is often compounded when someone has come from a dance style such as salsa where they are used to only dancing a single track and say "Thank-you!" and then happily walk away.

Fortunately, more experienced dancers will usually look at the context. If you're dancing with a beginner who clearly enjoyed themselves, then something as simple as *"In tango we usually dance for three songs"* with a smile, will get an enthusiastic response. If you don't say anything, but they've come with a more experienced friend, they may well promptly send them back to you!

This is the one time I'll offer unsolicited advice in a milonga. If they've said "thank-you" at the end of each dance and are still there at the end of the tanda. I'll have a conversation with them like this.

Follower "That was great, thank-you!"

Me, smiling "You're very welcome. Would you like a piece of advice that'll help you a lot?"

Follower "Yes, please."

Me "In tango, saying 'thank-you' after a song actually means 'I don't want to dance with you any more' "

Follower "Oh! Really? I didn't mean..."

Me "No, I know, it's fine. I enjoyed dancing with you. I just wanted to let you know"

Follower "Thanks. Wait, I mean..."

Me "Ha, yes, it's strange isn't it? At the end of the tanda, 'thank-you' just means 'thank-you'. "

Follower "Oh great, thanks."

How tandas vary

Some DJs choose to have all their tandas have the same number of songs. Others group the tangos into fours and the valses and milongas in threes. Some appear to lose track of how many they've played and the numbers become random, while a special few follow a logic that is imperceivable to anyone but them...

There is a general consistency of playing the tandas in the order of two tango tandas, then either a tanda composed entirely of either vals or entirely of milongas, followed by another two tango tandas and then finally, another milonga or vals tanda (whichever wasn't played earlier in the sequence). So, either, "Tango, tango, vals, tango, tango, milonga", or "tango, tango, milonga, tango, tango, vals". Often written as TTVTTM, or TTMTTV, for short. Whichever sequence they chose, then repeats throughout the night. It will usually reset to the beginning of the sequence if the social dancing is interrupted for more than a few minutes, such as by a performance or for a special one-off tanda such, as salsa.

Often, between each tanda, there's a short burst of music called a cortina, which signifies, that yes, the DJ has finished this tanda. Ideally the cortina bears no resemblance to either the music that was in the tanda, or indeed any kind of tango music. Some DJs will play clips of adverts, or rock 'n' roll, for example. This doesn't always work, especially in venues that play nuevo music, which can lead to "Is this the cortina?" discussions between dancers. The length of the cortina also varies from DJ to DJ and can be anywhere from ten seconds to a minute. They are usually consistent though, so once you know how long one takes, then it should be that long throughout the milonga.

There is a tendency to think of asking for dances as being connected to the cortina. It makes sense. It's unlikely people will stop dancing together mid-tanda, so the most likely time that people will be available is at the cortina. Some like to wait until they've heard with beginning of the next tanda before making a decision whether they want to dance it and with whom. Some accept provisional invitations during the cortina.

Others trust the DJ and are happy to accept invitations during the cortina. Some people just want to dance and really don't care about the music involved...

It's easy to get into the habit of only asking during, or just after the cortina. In reality, you can ask someone at any time. One of the classic risk-averse techniques for asking strangers is to do so when there's one song left of the tanda. If it goes well, you can say, "Shall we see what the next tanda is?" If it goes horribly, you just say, "Thank-you" and go and find someone else.

DJs tend to adjust what they're playing depending on the room. So at the beginning of the evening, the first milonga tanda will usually be the kind of milonga that if you looked on the back of the cd, would say "milonga/tango". It's basically a "diet" milonga you can tango to instead, if you or you partner aren't that confident about dancing milonga, or don't recognize it as a milonga. Some DJs may even skip the first milonga tanda in the sequence entirely, giving TTTTVTTM. Others deliberately go with TTVTTM so that the milonga has been going for over an hour before the first milonga tanda.

This is because the beginning of a milonga, is mostly attended by the less experienced dancers who have done the class. To compound this, generally, tango dancers prefer not to chose milonga for their first tanda, or with someone they don't know. As the DJ is trying to get people onto the floor to dance, it makes no sense to risk scaring them off with milongas.

The same reasoning is why more complicated and challenging music, usually isn't played at the Beginning.

As it's often quieter at this stage and so people can be less fussy about who they dance with. This is useful if you want to dance Competitive people who don't want to be seen dancing with you by a specific person, but that person doesn't usually turn up till later and so isn't an issue right now. It's also a time when people warm-up and aren't at their best, so "charity" dances are much more common.

The Gender/Role balance can shift through the evening and vary significantly between venues. Although in milongas, women usually outnumber the men, the most likely time for there to be more men than women is at the beginning. When this happens, it becomes much more likely that the men start looking for dances earlier in the cortina and will actively go to women they know, or met during the class. If there are more women than men at the Beginning, it may stay that way throughout the night, or it may come back into balance as more women arrive, but most likely later in the evening, the situation will reverse and there will be more women than men. So as a man, if you've arrived at the Beginning, a simple option if you're not used to having to compete for women and don't want to, is to simply leave the milonga with some friends and go and grab a coffee nearby for half an hour, or so.

Unfortunately for women, I can't remember a single time when I've been to a milonga that had more women than men to start with and then either came into equilibrium, or tipped over into there being more men than women. I can't even remember anyone telling me about such a thing happening. I mean, it must happen, surely?! If you're new to an area or a venue, it might be worth giving it the benefit of the doubt and going to get some coffee with your friends for a while. But, you probably want to prepare yourself for it staying that way for the rest of the night.

The Middle

If you arrive in the Middle, things are already in motion. It's much more likely that the people you know will have turned up and will dance with you to get you going.

Now that more people are here, this is when it's more likely to have situations when there are more women than men.

Different leaders react in different ways to there being a lot more women than men. Some, as one follower put it, "start strutting around like little Pablo Verons." Others find it stressful trying to deal with the logistics. There's about five tandas each hour. So if you're at a milonga for two hours, that's about ten tandas, assuming you dance all of them. So what is a leader to do if there are eleven women there who they know well and who all want dances as followers? What if there's twenty!

Let's take a look at what you can do and perhaps more importantly what your fellow followers can do. This is where we start getting into "the other women are the enemy."

You can apply all the same techniques you'd use under normal circumstances. The question becomes, are you just looking out for yourself? There will often be an uneasy alliance among the followers as they try to be seen to be sharing the leaders. But it doesn't take much to break this détente, either. One woman actively stalking and pouncing may raise some eyebrows and garner a few tuts. But if a few more join in, then the energy of the place can shift dramatically.

A telling sign this has happened is when you see men dancing together who don't normally do so. They're probably feeling harassed to the point that if they sit down with a drink, women will still come and verbally ask them. Sometimes dancing with each other is literally the only safe place in the room! Of course, it just makes the whole matter worse for the women, who understandably tend to react by thinking "There are only few guys here and now they're dancing with each other!"

Under these circumstances, the two men dancing together will almost always clearly be a farce, because they're just blowing off steam and relaxing, which tends to annoy the women further!

Women who can lead, will tend to start doing so, even if they didn't intend to when they came out, which helps a bit. You can usually tell in this situation, by looking at their shoes. If they're leading while wearing heels, they probably intended just following when they left home, whereas flats or Greek sandals mean it's far more likely they were either prepared for the possibility of too many women, or came wanting to lead.

The End

Depending on where you are, what day it is and when the milonga finishes, the last tram/train/bus times and getting up for work in the morning are big factors whether you want to stay until the end.

There's also the issue of the last tanda/dance, which has recently got more complicated. There's a general acceptance that if you came with your significant other, you should dance the last dance with them.

This used to be La Cumparsita *(la kuum-par-SEE-tah – traditionally the last song played to signal the end of the milonga)* and was played at the end of the last tanda. Some DJs will helpfully yell out "Last tanda!"

or "último tanda!" during the last cortina.

Although it should be obvious when this is, (about ten to fifteen minutes before the end of the milonga) sometimes DJs overrun. I've seen people who realized they weren't getting a dance for what they thought was the last tanda, get changed and start to say their goodbyes, only to discover when that tanda ended, the DJ had actually over-run. Then, when the DJ started to play another cortina, and announced "Last tanda!" they were left standing there helplessly.

But as I say, things have got more complicated. Some DJs have stopped playing La Cumparsita as the last track. Some will even play it halfway through the evening! Now in theory, this isn't a problem. The last tanda is still the last tanda, right? (Unless they over-run...) Well, it would be, if it weren't for the DJs who play the last tanda without La Cumparsita, then a cortina and then play La Cumparsita on its own!

And sometimes the DJs who always say "Last tanda" get distracted and forget...

Still not complicated enough? Well it's also common for the other DJs who end their last tanda without La Cumparsita, to then signal "We're done, go home" by playing cortina music. So if you don't know what this specific DJ does, and the what you thought was the last tanda, didn't end with La Cumparsita, what do you do when the next cortina starts? It feels annoying similar to waiting for the end-of-movie credits, in case there's a bonus scene. Indeed, there will often be a lot of furtive looking around to see what everyone else is doing.

The romantic significance of La Cumparsita

It's generally considered good etiquette to dance La Cumparsita with your significant other, though if you don't have one to hand, this can include your platonic dance partner or friend. La Cumparsita used to be a part of the last tanda, so by extension, you danced the last tanda with your significant other. Now people are left wondering, is it that you can dance the last tanda with anyone and then find your Significant Other for La Cumparsita, or do you do dance both with them?

To complicate things even further, some solve this dilemma by dancing what might be the last tanda with anyone and then bail if La Cumparsita comes on. Which will occasionally get them withering looks from the friend they didn't dance with, who's now fully changed out of their tango shoes, but would have happily danced the whole thing with them.

Bailing on someone is overkill. While La Cumparsita has some romantic significance, it's still perfectly acceptable to dance it with a stranger, without there being any strings attached. It's more your first choice should be to dance it with your significant other, rather than anyone you dance it with automatically becomes you significant other. Even this isn't written in stone. I've known husbands accept the last tanda with someone who wasn't their wife, and said wives, having raised an arched eyebrow and given them a look, then invited me to dance.

If you're single, you can largely assume this is someone else's problem. It makes sense for significant others to simply go and sit next to each other during the cortina that's before the last tanda (or their best guess of when this is) and not bother looking for invitations.

Let's assume it's near the end of the milonga and you've got a tanda with someone who doesn't have a significant other, the DJ's just finished playing four songs, the tanda hasn't ended with La Cumparsita and cortina music is being played. You say "Thanks", smile, and go back to your seat to get changed. You've got one of you shoes off, and then hear the beginning of La Cumparsita...

If you want to dance La Cumparsita with them, the easiest thing way to avoid the above situation, is to start talking about the tanda you just had and the night in general. If you can kill thirty seconds (often considerably less), either it will become obvious that the evening has ended (and the lights will probably be switched on) or La Cumparsita will begin. Even if you only kill twenty seconds and they wander off, be aware of the possibility of still getting the last dance with them, if it comes on and they realize. They'll almost certainly be happy to dance with you, because they're unlikely to get back to their seat and take their shoes off in under ten seconds, let alone find someone else. Walking them back to their seat will further kill time and place you practically next to them if La Cumparsita starts.

If they immediately say thank-you, pat you on the arm and wander off, forget it. Though there's nothing to stop you asking someone else to dance La Cumparsita if it comes on. Again, if you're not sure what's going on with the cortina, you can go and talk to someone about the night for a few moments and see what happens.

How to feel more welcome at milongas

If you feel that milongas are scary places, something that may change your mind, is to go to a venue and try to say, "Hi" to everyone there. While this may seem like a terrifying idea, it's worth doing once, as it will give you a very different perspective. Hopefully afterwards, you'll realize that milongas are, on the whole, filled with relatively normal people, rather than unfriendly lunatics. Doing this at a Cooperative venue can restore your faith in humanity.

You can also do this with a friend. Make it your mission to say, "Hi" to everyone. A friend and her cousin went a step further and added the rule that any time they ended up talking to someone, they had to make up fictitious stories about who they were. And they couldn't repeat those stories later on. While I gather alcohol may have been involved, making it into a game, rather than "Facing your fears!" makes it much easier.

Oxytocin, your new best friend

Eventually you'll hear or read something about "oxytocin", the "cuddle drug", and tango. The short version is that it's released when you cuddle someone and gives you that warm fuzzy feeling. So there's an obvious link to dancing in close embrace, especially the style known as "cuddle-shuffling".

However, the longer version will make your tango experience much better, even if you don't dance in close embrace.

Something that puzzled me for a long time, was that at one specific venue, I'd dance with a follower, R, and get what I now recognize as an oxytocin high. But at other venues, it was never as strong. Which made me wonder, what was I doing differently?

The emotions that you feel, are caused by various chemicals in your bloodstream. But you don't have that many of them, so they often do double-duty. The difference between fear and excitement, is a fine line. Both involve adrenalin. Indeed, adrenalin junkies get excited from doing things that invoke fear.

Oxytocin is actually first released into your blood, when you feel stressed, along with adrenalin. It causes you to seek social comfort from others. When you do this, you get the warm fuzzy feelings. Nature also entices people to give you social comfort, by giving them a hit of the oxytocin warm and fuzzies if they give you comfort. This is why when something stressful happens, we tend to go to our friends to talk about it, hug a teddy bear, write it in a diary, or pray to benevolent beings. We're trying to shift from the feeling of being stressed, to the oxytocin pay-off.

A non-tango example of this is when you're walking to your car with two bags full of shopping and they chose that moment to tear, sending tins merrily rolling around the floor. You immediately feel stressed. A compassionate stranger seeing your plight will feel moved to help you. They'll also feel somewhat stressed, at approaching a stranger, even if it's to help. But once you realize they're helping you and they realize you're grateful, you both get a hit of oxytocin and immediately feel better about each other and the situation.

The relationship between oxytocin and adrenalin also explains why people at raves have a ridiculous amount of energy. Yes, they're often out of their minds on oxytocin, hugging everyone and telling them how much they love them, but they're also up on adrenalin and so can bounce along all night long. In a room of like-minded people, you don't need drugs to do this.

There's also the possibility of the double-hit. Imagine that you and your friend are both stressed and both give each other comfort. You each get a hit of oxytocin from the other's comfort. However, you also both get another hit from successfully offering the other comfort. A simple example of this in tango is floorcraft. Someone bumps into you, causing you and your partner to be momentarily stressed. You both mutter something comforting to the other, like "Sorry" and provided you do a good job, you both get a double-hit of oxytocin. If you take a moment to socially comfort the couple who bumped into you and they reciprocate, there's even more oxytocin to go around!

And it gets better. When you enter into this exchange of social comfort, your body also releases dopamine and serotonin. Dopamine makes you feel more positive and increases your ability to do physical tasks, such as dancing, while serotonin boosts your perception and intuition, again both of which are very useful when dancing. It also calms down your amygdala, reducing any fear or desire to avoid others you may be feeling. This helps to explain why someone can be jittery when you begin to invite them, but they then start to relax and become more welcoming as this tango cocktail starts to get to work.

This works with anyone who reciprocates social comfort with you, whether they're your Nurturing partner, the people in your Competitive group, friends, strangers or random shiny people.

There is however, a missing element. Your body reacts to stress in one of two ways. If you think that stress is bad, then as well as releasing various chemicals, your blood vessels will constrict, making it harder for your heart to pump blood around your body. But, if you think that stress is good (bear with me!) you still get the same chemicals released, however, your blood vessels don't change. Research shows that which reaction you get, is simply a matter of what you believe. So if someone bumps into you and you think "Oh good, some oxytocin. I'll feel all warm and fuzzy if I get some social comfort", then, strange as it seems, you'll find the whole experience rather pleasant.

This applies to all the things that make a milonga stressful. If someone rejects you, you get a burst of oxytocin. The next person to accept your dance will then get warm and fuzzies for helping you. And you'll also receive them, because your invitation was accepted. If the DJ is playing awful music, or the numbers are imbalanced, or everyone seems hostile, in fact anything that makes you stressed at a milonga, it's fine, this is just a shot of oxytocin which is going to pay off. This is "good" stress. You can even use it with that "unapproachable" dancer. If you feel stressed that someone thinks you're not good enough, you can take that stress and oxytocin and get the "rush" with someone else entirely.

There's a "comfort zone" within which you can deal with good stress without being overwhelmed, which will gradually expand with practice. If you need to reduce the amount of good stress you're feeling and you can't get social comfort fast enough, you can use other concepts from this chapter to help reduce it to something more manageable.

One of the hidden keys to successfully understanding invitations, is recognizing whether the person you're inviting is under good stress, or bad stress, and how much oxytocin is involved. Someone under the influence of the warm fuzzies, or good stress (or both!) is a pleasure to invite. Good stress tends to give a definite clarity to the process, and oxytocin adds warmth and a feeling of wanting to do this. The experience of inviting someone undergoing bad stress, is rather different. They can be jittery, often second-guessing themselves whether you're inviting them, if they're good enough, or even if they feel like dancing. Assuming you manage to invite them, how well the dance will go, will depend a lot on converting the bad stress into an oxytocin hit. For this to work, you have to want the other person to be comfortable. So, acting judgmentally, or dancing in a way that's awkward for them, won't go well.

The best thing you can do in all these cases is to slooooow down your invitation. Dancers on an oxytocin high, tend take a bit longer anyway. Those under good stress, will enjoy stretching out the invitation in an almost cat-like way. Those under bad stress will find it easier to accept if you calmly give them a little extra time.

Be aware of your own state when inviting people. If you're undergoing bad stress, you'll probably be less clear and more jittery. Two people undergoing bad stress and trying to invite each other is going to be hard work. In some cases, you may need to chat a little, or give each other a "hello hug", before you embrace.

Two people slowly inviting each other, while under both good stress and oxytocin, will feel like they're having a magical moment all to themselves.

Let's go back to those thrill-seeking adrenalin junkies. There are things that make them afraid in a bad way, so what's the difference? In simple terms, it comes down to whether you view the situation as a threat, or as a challenge that you can overcome? Threats make you feel bad, especially if you don't think you can deal with them. Challenges however, when you feel you can overcome them, produce "good stress".

Knowing this, I now realize in retrospect, the reason I got such a high from dancing with R at that one venue, was that, at the time, we both found it a very stressful place, bordering on out-right hostile at times. So when we danced in close embrace, and she knew I would keep her safe, we both got a very strong double-dose of oxytocin. Whereas, when we danced in the more serene venues, where we didn't feel anywhere near as stressed, and this didn't happen.

OLIVER KENT

Chapter 9 - Using the cortina's dead air to your advantage

"Sssh. Don't tell anyone this. This is a secret."

~ Jay Rabe

When the cortina begins, there's usually a period of dead air, where, as far as getting dances is concerned, nothing constructive happens. This may even involve the entire cortina for those who want to wait until hearing the beginning of the music before making any decisions. Or it may just be a part of it, enough to remove the awkwardness of inviting someone to dance and then having to make small talk for another twenty seconds.

Many will just sit and wait, or chat to each other, until it's over and time to take action. However, there are a number of things, especially the techniques from Chapter 6, that you can do during this dead air to make you significantly more successful with your invitations.

Onomatopoeia

Have you ever seen someone approach you at a milonga, who looked like they were going to sound suitably confident, but when they first spoke, it was more of a squeak, whisper, or boom? You may have experienced squeaking yourself.

This can happen when the person about to talk, hasn't spoken to anyone for a while. This is especially true if they have conversations in their head, where their voice sounds normal and confident and so they can misjudge the volume needed to speak and project to someone "in the real world".

Despite being a social dance, there are a surprising number of times in tango when you'll find you haven't been talking for a while. In particular, you probably don't have an ongoing conversation while you're dancing a tanda. Or you may have been sitting out a tanda, on your own, in silence. These can lead to you squeaking as you speak to someone for the first time, whether it's a verbal invitation, or you've just done the cabeceo ritual and are now asking them to dance, or you're simply saying "Hi" to someone.

A simple solution to this, is to use onomatopoeia. When you're on your own during dead air, simply say "Dum, da-da-dum" along to whatever music is playing. Pronouncing actual "words" is an important part of this process, so humming doesn't work as well. The first time you try this, you may well feel self-conscious, in which case, start quietly. You'll be surprised how much background noise there is during the cortina, with the combination of people talking and moving around, bar-staff clinking glasses and the music. This lets you gradually raise your volume, while still being able to keep it hidden under the background noise. Doing this, helps you more precisely gauge just how loudly you'll need to speak when you do want to be heard. You can also fine-tune the energy you're using as you "Da-dum", whether to make it more calm, happy, bouncy or whatever suits your personality.

Pre-emptive Glancing

Similarly, when you haven't made eye contact in a while, you can re-adjust and fine-tune, by looking around the room using soft focus and Where did they put my cereal? The mirada is too intense and overt for dead air and can lead to accidental "premature cabeceoing". Just look around the areas of those dancers that you're interested in. But take your time. You don't want to look like a Prom Queen with OCD on crack cocaine. You can also start by looking in the area of your first preference, if you have one, then look to areas around others, and finally return to looking around your first choice again, as the dead air is about to end.

One of the big problems with looking at people at this stage, is judging how far you can clearly read someone's interest, under whatever conditions you find yourself in. Lighting, people moving around and so forth, can have a significant effect.

By just glancing around the room, you'll probably make unintentional eye contact with someone for a moment. The kind that gives you that slight spark of recognition that you've been seen. It's exactly the same that you experience on public transport, or if you look around a restaurant. This now gives you a much clearer marker for how far you can cleanly make eye contact. These sparks, also help to warm you up, so that when you next make eye contact with someone, it doesn't jolt you as much.

In moderation, this process generates a certain degree of (hopefully) good stress in all involved. After the dead air, you can then cash this in for a hit of oxytocin, as you both go through the process of accepting each others' invitations.

Choosing the right distance for both of you

When it comes to looking at people and gauging their interest in you, there are five ranges. Again, they vary due to eyesight, how well lit the milonga is, etc.

They are:

Too far,

Not quite close enough to be sure,

Not close enough to be sure until you do it successfully,

Close enough to be certain,

Too close.

Different readers will place those categories at different places among the images below. Some venues will have their own ideas on where these distances are, perhaps insisting that you cabeceo from across the room, or that go directly over and verbally ask. The person you're looking at may also have significantly different ranges to you.

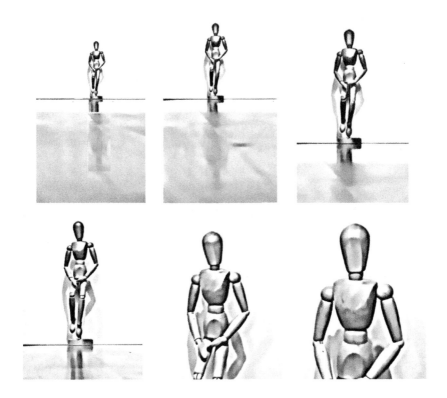

If you feel you're either too far away, or too close, simply move to a better distance. But pay attention to how the other person is behaving. If they seem to be straining to see you, move closer. If they seem to be uncomfortable with you being that close, move further away. If you're both in the not quite close enough to be sure range, fiascos can ensue, as neither of you will ever get to the point of being certain enough to take definite action.

I've once seen this go on with my friend who was sitting next to me, for the length, not only of the cortina, but also of the entire first song! When it became clear this was going to carry on throughout the tanda, I gave up and waved to the poor guy and beckoned him over. It turned out he was trying to cabeceo the woman next to her, but at least they finally got to dance and everyone was put out of their collective misery. In retrospect, one of them should simply have got up and moved into the close enough to be certain range.

Positioning

Sometimes, due to the layout of the milonga, you simply can't position yourself at the optimum distance. It might be there's a fire exit there, or you'd have to stand in front of someone's table, and so forth. For this situation, much like the Magician's Trick, simply walk as if you are going to somewhere reasonable. It might be a seat, it might be the bar. But you're going to time your journey, so that as the dead air ends, you'll be at the optimum place to invite the dancer you wanted to, allowing you the opportunity to pause and do so, rather than continue to your supposed destination. If they decline, then simply carry on with your journey.

While people may object to you standing in front of their table for half the cortina, no-one will object to you simply walking past it, so using this method gives you a lot of freedom to walk around the outside of the dance floor, or even across it, in order to get to a better position.

If you're interested in several dancers and they're spaced out, you can also move around the room during the dead air period, looking around each dancer in turn, as you reach each optimum place to do so. This is particularly useful in venues that are oddly shaped, or have obstructions such as columns, where choosing to remain in one position will prevent you from being able to see all the dancers you're considering.

When first trying to appraise someone's interest, most assume that it makes sense to sit directly opposite the person. That way, you're both looking directly at each other and it avoids confusion. There are two potential problems with this. Due to the layout of the room, they may be too far away.

However, even if they're at a more comfortable distance, it's often too intense to be sitting opposite someone and looking in their general direction for the dead air part of the cortina. You run the risk of generating too much stress and both of you feeling increasingly uncomfortable, resulting in bad stress for both of you and all the problems that causes (Chapter 8). Try looking at the picture below for twenty seconds and then imagine what that would be like with a real person in a milonga during dead air.

Even when they're looking to the side, it's still too much and lacks the subtlety required for this stage. This can lead to you actively trying to not look in their direction while you wait for the dead air to finish, which can then be mistaken, for you having lost interest in them.

Diagonals and Peekaboo

By placing yourself at a diagonal, you avoid this initial problem. As an additional benefit, it will be clearer to both of you when it comes time to invite, if you both chose to turn to face each other, as in the picture to the right.

It also makes it easier to look around and consider a number of people you would be interested in dancing with, as very few people will be directly opposite you. Do this in a relaxed way, as if you'd lost track of where your friend has got to and you're looking for them.

You can just gaze around the room in one continuous panning motion. Alternatively, you can look from point to point. Or a mixture of the two. You also don't have to look around the room in one direction. You can jump around, first look nearby to your right, then further away to your left, then maybe sweep across back to the right again. And so on.

At this point, you're not too concerned whether they respond. Again,

135

because of the nature of dead air, they're probably not going to want to get caught in the awkward feeling of looking back at you for a prolonged period, right now. What may happen instead, is that you look around them and then look at somewhere else further away. This allows them to then look around you and look away. At which point you again look around them, and so on.

You can continue this "plausible denial" version of "peekaboo" until the dead air ends, at which point, confidently invite them. Playing peekaboo cycles through creating a small amount of good stress, then releasing it into oxytocin, creating increasing feelings of warmth and trust in each other, as you take it in turns to look in the other's direction. This will significantly pay off when you embrace. It's also a lot more pleasant than just staring at the floor during dead air.

If you don't get some kind of response, don't make the mistake of looking continuously in their area for a protracted length of time. It's tempting to fall into the trap of believing that they just haven't looked your way yet and the moment you look away, will be when they look at you, and on seeing you looking elsewhere, they'll abandon all hope, causing you to lose your opportunity to dance forever! Fortunately it doesn't work this way.

Even if you don't want to dance with anyone else for the next tanda, if you're not playing Peekaboo, then deliberately take a break and periodically look around the rest of the milonga. At this stage, no response isn't necessarily a bad thing. They may simply not know it's possible to act during the dead air. Or they might be a lot better at being subtle about it than you are at the moment.

Because this stage tends to be much more subtle, if they don't appear to be looking back, it might be they've used their peripheral vision to notice you looking in their direction and intend acting on it once the dead air is over. Or they may have decided they want to try to see if they can garner interest or invitations from someone else first, before you. Or it could be they're sufficiently confident that you intend inviting them and so are going to feign nonchalance until you do so. The more comfortable you get with these techniques, the more inviting will shift from some terrifyingly confusing act, to something far more sophisticated and playful.

As the dead air comes to an end

The more subtle nature of the behavior during dead air can also act to provide a much stronger contrast with "taking action" as it ends. The follower who might have looked in your direction a couple of times while she was talking with her friend has now stopped talking, turned to face you and is giving you her best "hopeful meerkat" impression. The leader who glanced your way a few times, but seemed more interested in the cute blonde on the other side of the room, is now walking towards you with a confident smile on his face. And so on.

At this point, you want to consider the reactions, if any, you've received from those you've glanced at, and decide upon your order of preferences. It's not going to be set in stone, especially if you're going to wait until the music starts to see who would best fit it. However, if you are happy to move, this is a good time to decide where you want to be in the milonga, and get to a position with better sight-lines. Or you can place yourself so that the person you want to verbally approach first, is closest.

If you are considering several people, place yourself to invite them in your order of preference. If you're subtle enough, you can appear to just be taking in who's there as your invitations are declined and give the "plausible" impression that the person who eventually accepts your invitation was the one you originally intended.

Try to avoid positioning yourself so that you'll have to walk clockwise around the ronda, especially at the same time as the other dancers are entering it for the next tanda.

What to do when several people you want to invite are sitting next to each other

At first glance, this seems like a horrible situation. If you ask the first person and they turn you down, surely the second person is going to be irritated if you then ask them, as they're clearly your second choice? This is again, where positioning comes in. There's two main factors to consider. The direction they're facing (which can change) and who's closest.

Approaching straight on with two people, who are also looking straight ahead, is usually your worst possible option. Try to avoid putting yourself in this position, shown in the picture below, either as the person approaching, or as one of those being approached. The most likely outcome, is that all three of you are confused, especially if they both want to accept your invitation.

If you place yourself so that as you make your invitation, the person nearest you is your first preference and they decline your invitation, there is plausible deniability that the reason you asked them was purely because they were closest, and not because they were a better choice. This allows you to then ask the next person and let them save face. It also gives the first person the opportunity to turn to face you, clarifying that they probably do want to accept.

If they turn away, but the person next to them turns to face you, that's a good indication to stop inviting the first person and instead invite the second.

In case you're worried that the person you invited second, will be grumpy for this tanda, usually the joy of getting to dance, outweighs the slight nudge to their ego. By the time you're settled into the embrace, they'll have forgotten about it.

If two people are talking together, rather than approaching them straight on and having them both look up at you expectantly, you can safely invite the one you want, from a position to the side and behind the one you're not interested in. In the first picture below, you want to invite the dancer on the right, so in the second picture, you've placed yourself behind and to your left of the person they're talking to, allowing the one you want to clearly show their interest in dancing with you, by turning more to face you.

It's also important to be mindful of how easy your positioning makes it for others to approach you. Another way to avoid putting yourself in the awkward situation of everyone looking straight forward, is to look in a different direction than the surrounding people, as shown in the picture below. This allows a much clearer invitation to be made along the direction you're looking in.

In the picture below, you're approaching from the left to invite the person on the right and they have placed themselves accordingly to make it easier to accept. You could equally have approached from the right, if you'd wanted to invite the dancer below on the left.

Because you're deciding ahead of time who you'd like to invite, it's statistically unlikely that all the people you want to dance with will be next to each other, unless they're in a group, in which case they'll be used to the idea of people inviting them one at a time.

If you do find yourself inviting three people close to each other (because the first two declined), it's wise to then move to another area of the milonga, before you continue inviting people. If you don't have anyone else in mind, take a moment, have a quick scan around and then decide if anyone appeals to you. This avoids the situation where you're clearly just asking everyone one after the other, in the hope of a dance. You can do that, especially in a co-operative venue, but if you do, you really need to own it.

Tables and Corners

Corners and tables behind tables, can severely limit your options. It depends a lot on the exact layout of the venue, but when in a corner, you often can't see along the two adjoining walls. One of the others may be too far away for effective eye contact. Of the remaining wall (unless the room is unusually shaped, such as in a bar), the space directly opposite you isn't great. So you can end up having really only one effective place for you to receive invitations from. Or indeed, no obvious places at all.

If you're trying to invite someone in an inaccessible position, it's again possible to use the technique of walking and timing your journey, so that as the dead air ends, rather than continue to your supposed destination, you're now at the optimum place to invite the dancer you want to, even if that position is one that would, under normal circumstances, be unavailable to you, such as the middle of the dance floor. Just look like you were crossing it to go to the bar and as the dead air ends, make firm eye contact. If they accept, for the benefit of anyone watching, just act as if they made eye contact with you and so you've changed you mind about going to the bar and are now going to them instead.

You can also wait for opportunities. I was at a milonga where one follower remained safely ensconced at a table behind a table, just emerging to dance with her two partners. However, halfway through the milonga, she went to talk to the DJ. I waited until she was almost finished and then started walking, as if I intended to go past the DJ and on further around the room. As she finished talking to the DJ and turned back towards the tables, the dead air period ended, I met her gaze and successfully invited her to dance. I was then able to get further tandas with her, later in the evening, by first looking around in her direction during the dead air (as well as glancing at other followers) and then as it ended, cabeceoed her from across the room, so that the tables no longer presented an obstacle.

This also works the other way around. If you want to significantly filter out the people who invite you, then you can deliberately place yourself where there's only one place for them to go to invite you. If they go there and look in your direction, it's a pretty good sign they're interested.

Some will take this a step further, choosing to position themselves so that the best place to invite them from is usually occupied. Or it may be awkward, whether that involves blatantly crossing the dance floor in a venue where no-one does that, or having an arduous trek around assorted people, columns and handbags in order to eventually get to them. Or even, only accepting the invitation when the music has started and then requiring their partner to navigate across the dance floor the wrong way around to get to them, as the other dancers begin the tanda.

If you realize that someone has placed themselves thus, ask yourself whether you think they're a Nurturing or Competitive dancer? People choosing to place themselves at inaccessible positions will often either compensate through more awareness, or are deliberately filtering, in which case you may need to use the appropriate strategy for their type.

In particular, if you see women sitting in a corner who then dance together, it's often a sign that the optimal places to invite them are pretty small and may well be obstructed.

Chapter 10 - Birthday valses

"… to a very dear sister.

A birthday of three big kisses:

XXX"

~ MsHedgehog

The "vals" is the Argentine tango equivalent of a waltz. It refers to both a style of dance that tends to be more lyrical and circular in movement, as well as a style of music.

Some venues celebrate a dancer's birthday with the aptly named, Birthday vals. The floor is cleared and everyone forms a loose circle around the edge. The person(s) whose Birthday it is, starts in the center of the dance floor and dances with one person, while a vals is played. The other dancers should be far enough away for the starting couple to dance, but also close enough for people to easily join in and exit back to the circle. At some point, another person will "cut in" and start to dance with the Birthday dancer.

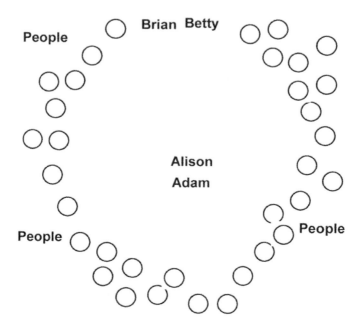

It's a good way to get seen, particularly if you're one of the people who does the cutting in and can result in you getting more and better dances later on that evening. (I got a raised eyebrow from a friend who read an early draft of this.

"*I thought this was supposed to be a 'treat' for the Birthday person(s)?*"

Well, yes it is. But this is a book about getting dances, so in this case you can have your cake and eat it.) You will however, want a reasonable amount of skill and a certain amount of courage to take part.

While this seems like it should be a fairly straight-forward process, let's look at the ways it can get a bit more complicated and what you can do to make your own life easier.

Getting started

If it's your Birthday and you would like a Birthday vals, you should speak to the teacher/organizer in advance of the event, as they may not be aware that it's your Birthday. You should arrange for a partner to start off the vals with you. If you're on your own, there's a reasonable chance the teacher themselves will dance with you, but it's polite to ask them ahead of time if they will partner you when the time comes. However, it's wise to also arrange a back-up plan for the first person you're going to dance with, in case "stuff happens".

The teacher/organizer will announce that it's your Birthday and that this is your Birthday vals. Ideally they will give some kind of instruction as to what this actually means, but don't count on it. If you haven't pre-arranged to dance with the teacher and you have no back-up partner there's a moment, that can last quite a long time, of you standing alone in the middle of the floor, waiting for someone to come and dance with you. And unfortunately, it's human nature that most people don't want to go first. This can be extremely awkward.

A friend and I still reminisce about the first time I met her. Her teacher "helpfully" announced it was her Birthday vals and at a venue that almost never has them, basically pushed her into the middle of the floor and then went back to minding the DJ. My friend been learning for a few months, and this was a Competitive venue that another friend refers to as "filled with sharks and marks". As it became clear that *no-one* wanted to go first, the look on her face was the epitome of a deer in the headlights. You do not want this to be you! (I, being me, on seeing she'd been unintentionally thrown under a bus, promptly walked onto the floor and started dancing with her. Things went fine after that. So it's not the end of the world if this happens, it can just feel like it for a few seconds.)

This is where having already agreed with someone that they will partner you in this situation helps a lot! If you think it's unlikely the teacher will dance with you, because for example, they're doing double duty as the DJ, or they just don't dance socially, then I'd recommend asking a friend you trust to be your first partner for the vals, to ensure you have "a person you walk onto the dance floor with".

Let's consider a scenario where it's Alison's Birthday and she's kept a firm hold of Adam's hand until the music plays for her Birthday vals and they start dancing.

Cutting in

At some point, someone else is supposed to "cut in." Let's say that Brian wants to. He steps on to the floor, cuts in to start dancing with Alison, while Adam calmly leaves.

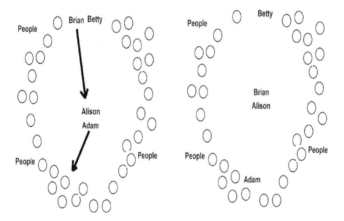

There's a number of complications with this. The first is simply how long are you supposed to wait until you cut in? It's feels fairly obvious when it's not been long enough, but the ideal time often has a feeling of uncertainty about it, followed by the realization that because no-one was quite sure, while they were all hesitating, it's now definitely become too long and is getting increasingly uncomfortable, which in turn makes people more hesitant *sigh*.

If you're really stuck for how long is right before cutting in, I'd say a slow count of 16 is a good measure. That's 4 counts for them to get adjusted to each other and 12 counts for the leader to exhaust their repertoire of flashy moves. Also, bear in mind, it's then going to take you some time to do the actual cutting in.

The main exception to this, when it's usually better to let things go on for a bit longer, is near the end of the song. Most people like to end on an impressive finish and frankly a lot of leaders need a bit of a mental run-up to accomplish that. Plus, it's not unusual for people to misjudge when the end is. But otherwise, err on the side of slightly too soon when cutting in.

There's a variety of ways you can cut in. At the end of the day, this is supposed to be fun, so don't get worried about using the Right Way. Personally I like to enter the dance floor when the leader is facing in my direction, or at least is likely to be turning to do so, for example, when they've just started a turn. I also like them to be a reasonable distance away. Walk confidently and slowly onto the floor and make eye contact with the leader. In an ideal world, all you have to do now is pay attention.

If the follower is the Birthday dancer, the leader should finish up whatever flashy moves they're doing and start positioning the follower so that they can make an easy transition to you. A common solution is simply to raise the follower's left arm (with the leader's right) as they release the embrace, causing the follower to do a gentle turn (think ballroom, Salsa or Modern Jive, rather than tango) and either step into the new leader's embrace, or exit the dance floor gracefully, depending on what's required of them.

If the leader is the Birthday dancer, they'll let their follower gracefully leave the embrace and let you embrace them. This usually works better they turn the follower before-hand so that the follower can see there's a new follower approaching.

Another option is to simply tap the leader on the shoulder and remain observant and close until the cutting in manoeuvre can be completed.

The most likely problem is that as you go to step onto the dance floor, someone else does too. Annoyingly, the most obvious solution does not work most of the time, so it's worth mentioning. What most people will instinctively do is an "After you" gesture and assume that they will in turn go after you. There may be a similar scene to that of two people trying to get through a door at the same time, but one of you will accept and that part will be fine. I don't know why, but 95% of the time, rather than let you go next, someone else will then decide to cut in ahead of you. This makes no sense to me, but I've seen it over and over, so there you go.

If you find yourself in this "After you" situation, either accept graciously and go first, or decline, knowing that it's really likely you'll have to wait awhile to cut in.

Generally, you only cut in once. The vals is intended to let the Birthday dancer enjoy the range of dances available. However, if it's a particularly quiet night, or people are hesitant about joining, then it's better to go back for a second time, than to leave it for so long that it starts becoming awkward that no-one seems willing to dance with the Birthday person.

If you're not the Birthday dancer, you can make your life significantly easier by doing one of two things. If you want to join in, make sure you're at the front of the circle of people and ideally have a bit of space around you. People leaving the dance floor during the vals will usually walk in a straight line and so can end up in front of you, inadvertently blocking you from joining in if you're slightly farther back. Conversely, if you absolutely do not want to join in, just put yourself at the back of the onlookers and you'll be left in peace.

The vals itself

The dancing itself is a strange animal. Following during a Birthday vals is one of the hardest things a follower can do. They have to keep adjusting to (often radically) different styles of lead and different moves, over and over again. In addition, leaders will tend to throw their flashiest moves at the follower in order to create a show for the onlookers, which the follower may not be fully expecting. If you're the follower in this situation, breathe and relax. At the end of the day, this is being done in a spirit of fun. If you mess up a move, DO NOT SHOW IT, just style it out and the leader should have the intelligence to pretend that whatever you just did, was what they intended.

If something goes completely wrong, laughing is a good get-out-ofjail card. With any luck the onlookers will laugh along with you. Likewise, if you're leading and you mess up, style it out and accept any help the follower gives you. In this respect, the Birthday vals is a bit more of a cooperative effort than pure social dancing.

If you're the Birthday dancer, don't assume someone is going to lead or follow based on whether they are a man or a woman, especially if they can do both roles, or if you can. It's entirely possible for men to dance with men and women to dance with women. It's also possible, just to add even more confusion to the mix, for them to expect you to change your role. So if you're a man who was leading, a woman may cut in and start leading you! (Though they will be confident that you can do the role reasonably well)! Be prepared for anything.

I'm going to be blunt and say that at the time of writing, women will almost always lead significantly better than men will follow. So if you find the person who cut in is a man who wants to follow, and you've never danced with him before, it's advisable to build in a lot of leeway to your leading to start with and don't take it too seriously. You may outshine the women, or it may turn into a farce. Accept whatever happens with good grace.

If you're cutting in and plan on doing the "opposite" role that your gender would imply, bear in mind, you've had time to adjust to this idea. It may take the couple you're cutting in on, a moment to realize and adapt. Also, be very clear which you prefer on joining. It's reasonable to quietly say "you lead" and offer your hand as a follower would during the small amount time it takes to change partners. Everyone will then be on the same page and the change-over will go more smoothly.

It's also possible, although unusual, for the Birthday dancer to refuse your offer of the "opposite" role. So I've seen a man dancing as a leader for his Birthday vals. Another man cut in expecting to follow, but instead the Birthday dancer opted to chose the follower's role himself.

Transitioning out

Generally, when the cutting in has been accomplished, there's a round of applause for whoever is leaving the dance floor, at least for the first few times. It makes life easier, so whether you intend participating in the dancing, I'd encourage you to join in with this.

To end your turn smoothly as a leader, as I mentioned, simply letting go and raising your left arm, so the follower does a spin either, into the arms of the next leader, or gracefully exits the floor, works well. The one problem with the whole arm raising spin, is that followers who have done modern jive, ballroom, salsa etc., will turn anticlockwise which is helpful. but those who haven't done any other dances will usually turn clockwise, which can be a lot messier and can cause problems if you're trying to pass them to another leader.

For this reason, when handing a follower from one leader to another, I'm a big fan of using the sandwich. (If you don't know what a sandwich is yet, you should probably hold off from leading in a Birthday vals until you do.) Lead and complete a sandwich, so that you're effectively in a block with your left foot to the follower' left and the follower is about to step over it with their right foot. The next leader simply stands at your right. You then gently guide the follower to step over and walk directly into the new leader's embrace.

You've got all the time in the world, and the follower can see exactly what's going on.

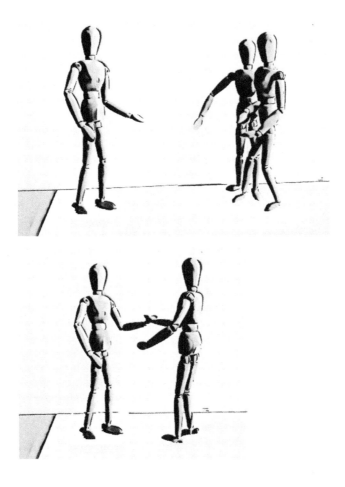

As a general rule of thumb, be aware of what's going on around you and help the other person you're dancing with be aware of anyone cutting in.

Don't rush.

Snowball vals

Another possibility is the Snowball vals. Sometimes, instead of one person cutting in, two people, a leader and a follower, usually a couple, cut in on the couple on the floor (leader to follower). One partners with the Birthday dancer, while the other dances with the remaining person (who was just dancing with the Birthday dancer.) Let's say it's Alison's Birthday and she starts dancing with Adam. Brian and Betty both cut in and now Brian and Alison are dancing together, as are Adam and Betty. The couple that includes the Birthday dancer stay roughly in the center and the second couple gives them some space.

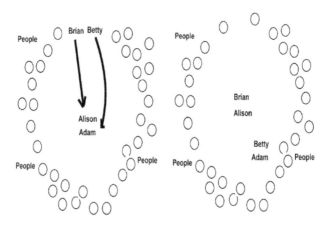

This continues with a new couple periodically cutting in to dance with the Birthday dancer and their current partner, until either, the whole room is dancing, or the song ends. It's a nice alternative in that it takes the pressure off everyone. The standard Birthday vals is rather a "center-stage spotlight shining on you" experience and so deters a lot of people.

The problem with this version is that if you want to join in, you need to convince someone to join in with you. This does get easier as the vals continues and the floor gets fuller and fuller, and everyone becomes less self-conscious. Unfortunately, this also means that fewer people will see you dancing and so the benefits of you joining in for the purposes of getting dances later on, also get smaller and smaller.

Snowball 2.0

There is another version of the snowball that is designed to be easier to join. In this version, Alison starts with Adam as before. In this version, only one person cuts in, so up to this point it's exactly the same as the normal Birthday vals. Brian cuts in and is now dancing with Alison. At this point, Adam, when he gets back to the edge of the dance floor, immediately asks someone else to dance, such as Claire and rejoins the floor with them, albeit, more off to the side.

I've never seen anyone refuse this invitation, as to do so would put the asker in a horrible position, though they could simply then ask someone else.

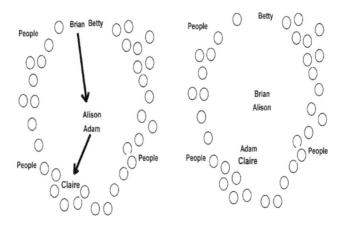

The process continues with a stream of single dancers periodically cutting in to dance with the Birthday dancer and their current partner then inviting someone else, until again, either everyone is dancing, or the song ends. Choose your partner wisely as you will be dancing with your partner for the rest of the track.

You'll find that, on the whole, Birthday valses don't really happen in Competitive venues, unless it's the Birthday of one of the "in-crowd". I've been to an event where there was a long performance, followed by a long speech. This in turn was then followed by a Birthday vals that only included the teachers, organizers and their close friends who were sitting at their table. It did not go over particularly well with the social dancers, who had to sit and wait for half an hour through all this! I've also turned up midway during another milonga as a similar extravaganza was just starting. Having waited for half an hour for it to end, I then heard someone come in and be charged less, as it was now past 11pm. I had literally paid extra for the privilege of standing for half an hour.

In Free Spirit venues, Birthday valses are quite popular. You can certainly help by bringing along a cake or treats, but it's not necessary. They do tend to be at the more disorganized end of the spectrum, but conversely, the better dancers will usually be happy to join in.

In Cooperative venues, they're almost a staple. Just mention it's your Birthday on the night, or send a message to the venue a few days before, and you're all set. In fact, I would advise this regardless – you never know what the organizers have in mind for a particular venue on a particular night and you're much more likely to be successful if you plan ahead.

Chapter 11 - Some thoughts about etiquette

"There is no substitute for good manners - except, perhaps, fast

reflexes."

~ Vlad Taltos

There are a lot of different points of view on tango etiquette. You can learn a lot about what's acceptable just by observing what goes on and quietly asking someone who's a regular, or who works there.

Consecutive tandas

Some people like the idea, some don't. It's more a matter of personal taste and a lot to do with where you lie on the scale of Cooperative – Nurturing. Pretty much, if you think it's a terrible idea, feel free to skip this bit. If you either like the idea, or would like to give it a try, read on...

You have a few choices when the first tanda you've danced together ends. You can stay in the embrace and see if they do. If you do this, I'd recommend doing one of two things. Firstly, don't stand completely still. It will just feel increasingly awkward, and you'll start wondering how a twenty-second cortina can be taking this long? Something as simple as gently weight-changing back and forth solves this problem. If you have a DJ who wants to do a minute long cortina, you can either start to match the weight-changes to the music, or very gently, start to go around in a circle. Talking is also an option, while staying in embrace.

Letting go can feel like a signal to break the embrace. An elegant solution to this, is just to let go with one hand and then re-establish the embrace with that hand. Then do the same with the other hand. This lets you both adjust and get comfortable, whilst killing some time. It also signals that you're both confident that the other wants to stay there and don't feel the need to keep hold of them.

Another choice, is that you can let go and keep talking. This is the lowest risk option. The other person can than chose to either keep talking with you, or they can just politely answer with a few words, say "Thanks" and then wander off. Women will often pat you on the arm when they do this, which is basically code for "I'm going, but I don't want to appear to be rude." So smile.

With both you can simply just ask, "Would you like/do you want, to rest or keep going?" or even "Another?" or "One more?" Indeed, with an enthusiastic partner, simply "More?" with a smile.

These work equally well with complete strangers, as they do with long-term dance partners.

As I mentioned at the beginning of this chapter, some people do not like the idea of multiple tandas. Again it goes back to the idea that "they mess up the economics of the milonga." By dancing with one partner for most of the evening, Competitive followers feel they get the leftover tandas, rather than being able to choose the tanda by an Orchestra that would inspire them both. Cooperative followers may be annoyed with the unfairness of someone having so many dances with one partner because it forced other people to sit out for longer than they should.

Both of them may also feel that dancing multiple tandas with someone, signals that they're a couple, or indeed are a romantic couple and are not available for other people to ask them. At the end of the day, there are rarely any actual Rules written down about this. There's certainly no enforceable Rule I'm aware of, that says if you dance consecutive tandas with someone you have to enter into a romantic relationship with them! But tempting as it may be, in my experience, you won't succeed if you try to explain this to the people who feel that dancing multiple tandas with you will cost them dances with others. They may also be getting tired of dancers taking it upon themselves to repeatedly ask if you're a couple.

Some will go even further and try to shame you into not dancing multiple tandas at all. The mildest version is making a fuss about clearing the floor between tandas, ostensibly because you're blocking their cabeceo. There's really only one of two ways this is going to be an issue.

Firstly, which frankly at the time of writing is going to happen 99% of the time, almost no-one is dancing consecutive tandas at this milonga. So realistically, even in a busy milonga, it's between zero and three couples who stay on the floor to dance the next tanda for any given cortina. If someone thinks **that's** the reason, they're not getting the dances they want, they really need to read this book. You can still work around this with the simple line "Ok, let's just stand off to the side so we're not in anyone's way." You can just brazen it out and stay there, though be aware that you may ruffle some feathers (although if you're a nurturing couple you may not care) and some milongas will have written rules about clearing the floor during the cortina (whether they actually enforce them is another matter.)

Or secondly, at this milonga, most people are dancing consecutive tandas, which case, that's just how things are done at this venue, so don't worry about it.

It's worth noting that people who don't dance consecutive tandas aren't evil either (or at least if they are, it's for other reasons.) Some people genuinely prefer to only dance one tanda at a time with the same person. So don't take it to heart if this happens. It's not an indictment of you, your dancing, or anything else.

Likewise, every once in a while, the stars and planets all align and someone break all their own rules and dance consecutive tandas, maybe with you, maybe with someone else. If it's with someone else, again, don't take it personally. If it's with you, don't assume that they'll ever do it again, though it doesn't hurt to ask.

Multiple Tandas

Multiple tandas are a slightly different issue. In this context, I specifically mean dancing more than one tanda with the same person during the milonga, but with a space of time between the tandas. An hour seems to be fairly well regarded as "a reasonable space of time". You'll often find that people who feel that consecutive tandas are a Thing of Evil, will be willing to dance multiple tandas with you throughout the evening. In particular, a reply you'll sometimes get when asking if someone wants to do another tanda, is "Later on." Provided it's said with a smile (and ideally they pat your arm), then take this at face value and follow it up later on, rather than thinking this is just someone politely turning you down.

Sometimes people will say variations of "Another later on?" at the end of a tanda without any prompting from you at all. Again, take these at face value.

Multiple tandas don't carry any implication of romance. They don't usually interfere with the economics of the milonga and the need to share, unless there's either a number imbalance, or that dancer knows a lot of people there who want to dance with them and barely has enough tandas to go around as it is.

The main way that multiple tandas are underused for getting dances is they can effectively halve the effort you spend looking for dances that evening. If you want, you can spend the second half of the evening just asking the people you've already danced with (and enjoyed dancing with!) earlier on. One of the less obvious benefits of this, is that you have more energy in the first half because you start reasonably fresh and haven't spent a lot of time dancing.

This means you can now pace yourself differently. Rather than having to keep reserves of energy for getting dances later on, you can just go for it during the first half of the evening. Be positive, and shrug off rejection. Because at the half-way mark, you stop trying. Sure, not all of those dances will yield a second tanda, but a good proportion of them probably will. And those dances in themselves will usually get you more dances with other people with minimal effort, as they see you dancing and that makes them want to invite and dance with you.

Claiming space

Groups accomplish this by having a semi-permanent presence in the milonga and usually one or two people who get there early. Otherwise, territory in milongas is remarkably fluid. Leave your seat to go dance, and it may not be yours any more when you return.

Should you escort her back to her chair?

Forget it with Free Spirits, though it's usually expected with Competitive dancers. It will tend to happen naturally with Nurturing dancers, while Cooperative dancers will often use it to introduce you to other people sitting near them. The big exception to all of this is the follower who wears glasses. They will often leave them on the table where you physically met them and may have difficulty getting back to the table unaided, not to mention finding / remembering where they put their glasses in the first place. In this case you should definitely escort them back.

Sweat

You are probably going to sweat while dancing tango. Frankly, you've already probably been sweating on the journey home from work and then from home to the milonga. The simplest answer is to have a shower before you leave home and apply some good antiperspirant deodorant.

For longer milongas, a small towel is a good idea, as is a plentiful supply of fresh shirts/t-shirts. You can go to the restrooms, dry yourself down and reapply the deodorant, especially in the Summer.

Take some spare t-shirts or shirts along with you to any dancing event you attend and change into a fresh one when it starts to get damp.

If you just stayed at home and watched a dvd, you'd probably have a snack and a drink at some point. Going to a milonga is a lot more energetic than watching a dvd! Bananas, before or after, will help replace the minerals you lose through sweating.

Smoking

With no-smoking laws rapidly gaining ground, increasingly there's a place outside where people go to smoke. It's also easy enough to go there simply to get some fresh air if you don't smoke. This is an easy way to talk to people without pressure and create connections that may get you dances later on. But if you come back in smelling of smoke, it may put some people off from dancing with you. Spraying scent on, changing your shirt and having some mints, can help to mitigate it. If you've danced with someone who smells of smoke, you can usually just wash it off in the restroom.

Scent

Honestly, there are people that will be put off if you bathe in scent. While I know people who like dancing with someone who smells nice, I'm not aware of anyone who finds it off-putting when someone isn't wearing any scent. Feel free to wear scent, just don't over-do it and don't think it will completely cover the smell of smoke, or bad body odor. Deodorant is always A Really Good Idea.

Breath mints

Mints, or indeed, brushing your teeth before you come out, is considered good etiquette, especially if you ate garlic for dinner. A lot of people drink during a milonga, so the effect of the mints wears off over the evening. You can keep topping it up, though you may find the combination of mint and what you're drinking isn't pleasant. I would not advise dancing whilst eating mints, though, as this can be a choking hazard.

Things in your pockets

This is a minefield. A lot of women's tango clothing either doesn't have pockets, or those that do are not very practical. Men's clothing tends to have pockets, but they're usually not designed with a close embrace/dancing in mind. It depends on the style that you dance, but generally the only place you can safely put your keys is in your back pocket, assuming you have one. Followers will not be pleased if you lead a wrap while you have your car keys in your trouser pocket. And close embrace is going to be unpleasant for both of you if you have them in your suit pockets, again assuming you're even wearing a suit to begin with. Leaving your wallet, phone and other paraphernalia in your pockets while you're dancing can be extremely uncomfortable for your partner.

Handkerchiefs are best left in your suit or back pocket. They're useful to have if your face is getting sweaty, especially in close embrace. You can simply dry yourself off between songs, though there is also a school of thought that it's rude for the man to dry himself with a handkerchief between dances when the woman can't.

Effects of water, alcohol and caffeine

Water will also help a lot. Bar Staff are obliged to give you free water from the tap, though these days you'll have to call it "tap water" or else they'll try to charge you for the bottled kind.

Some venues will have jugs of water, a supply of disposable plastic cups and some permanent marker pens. The idea being that you write your name on your cup and voilà, it's yours. If you don't want to broadcast your name, just use a symbol, such as a musical note or smiley face :) . I'm wary enough that once a glass or cup has left my sight, I'm not going to go back to it. I've never heard of anything untoward happening, in terms of people drugging drinks at milongas, but I have seen people cheerfully drinking other people's drinks, including mine which was clearly labelled as such.

There's a reason most milongas have a bar, or let you bring your own alcohol. In the first draft, I pointed out that a lot of people drink at milongas to help them relax and better cope with the social situation, and so dance better. I received another raised eyebrow from my friend over this.

"A lot of people *think* that they dance better when they've had some alcohol, when in fact the reverse is true. Alcohol will give you a false sense of confidence and reality. I would advise caution and say that most people enjoy the dancing too much, such that they do not feel the need to consume alcohol to relax and have a good time – but hey, that's me!"

Even if you feel it takes the edge off being nervous about the social situation, talking to strangers and so on, there's a tipping point where if you continue to drink alcohol, you'll start to notice your dancing getting worse.

In its various forms, caffeine gives you a weak jolt of adrenalin which gradually wears off and uses up your blood sugar in the process. Bringing along a bar of chocolate to replenish this can help. Some milongas will also provide cakes.

"I haven't danced in ages, sorry if I'm awful."

This is a great lead-in to a dance that will lower expectations and take the pressure off both of you, but can only be used if it's true. Surprisingly, it's pretty likely you'll be better than you expect. Often taking a break lets your subconscious work on things and you come back refreshed and a better dancer with new insights. You may well find that some kinks you had previously, have worked themselves out.

Talking while you dance

Some people love it, while others hate it. Some do it when the music is terrible and they'd rather catch up with their friend while dancing, rather than sitting down. It's one of those things where just because you see someone else doing it, doesn't mean that it'll work for you. Tread softly.

Singing

I've yet to meet a woman willing to sing while she dances who wasn't good at it. Not all leaders share my opinion, although I am aware that some leaders also enjoy singing while they dance. It can detract from the dance and make your partner feel you care more about the music than them, or it can add to the experience if you get lost in the music together. I would advise you first become comfortable with your partner, before you start singing along.

Chapter 12 – Festivals and Marathons

"After that tanda, I found that every man I danced with that evening had something beautiful to offer."

~ Carole McCurdy

At the time of writing, there are basically two types of "weekender" events. The names are becoming increasingly interchangeable, so check their website carefully and ask around.

Marathons tend to be round-the-clock continuous events. Music is played all the time. If you want to dance at 6am, you can. Or at least, there will be a milonga with music playing at 6am. Whether anyone's in it, is another matter, but you can experience a lot of dancing at a Marathon. One follower, at the height of her kid-in-a-sweet-shop phase, managed to dance a total of over 24 hours at one Marathon!

A Festival usually has a number of milongas scheduled throughout it. There may also be workshops and other forms of entertainment, such as film showings. As a rule of thumb, the opening milonga is the one a lot of people either won't turn up to, or will turn up late. Usually, it just means they didn't want to, or couldn't take the day off work. Anyone who's travelled a significant distance is probably getting over that. This tends to be more of a "pre-milonga" where friends say "Hi", and everyone starts to get into the mindset of the Weekend of Tango.

The last milonga of the Festival, also may not be so well attended, as people who have to travel, may have to leave early to catches trains, planes and so forth. This is the one where everyone's pretty much exhausted. The atmosphere tends to be much more chilled and relaxed.

Saturday evening will be the busiest. As the weekend progresses, people often prioritize dancing first with those they've met before, so it tends to be later in the event that people then start to look for new people to dance with.

Marathons generally follow these patterns too.

When it comes to getting dances, wearing distinctive jewelry and sitting in the same place, can help significantly, as there can be a lot of new faces to keep track of. If someone knows they're looking for the woman with the pink flower in her hair, or the man with the gold angel pin, they stand a much better chance of finding you, especially if you've spent the whole weekend in roughly the same spot. Conversely, if things haven't gone well, you can often get a fresh start by deliberately changing your look and sitting somewhere else.

Finding the one for you

I know several people who have got fed up with their news outlets giving them biased information, and so they go and buy foreign papers and peruse foreign news websites to get a more accurate picture of what's really going on. Similarly, if you're thinking of going to a Festival or Marathon, it's a good idea to ask around and not just rely on information from their website and the associated "In-crowd."

What's it going to be like for you? Does it have a reputation for being cliquey, or is it as one friend put it, "A bunch of hippies!" Are you going to be able to travel to and from your accommodation, especially late at night on a weekend? Is the venue intended for dancing? A marble floor may make for beautiful photographs, but everything in your body will not be happy after a few hours dancing on it, especially if you're wearing heels.

Do you get the impression it's Nurturing, Cooperative, Competitive or Free Spirit, because they all exist. What suits you? I know someone who was very happy to go from being one of the better followers in her city, to a Competitive Festival in another country where she was one of the worst and would get significantly fewer dances because of that, because she saw it as an opportunity to improve. For others, sitting out for most of a Festival would be a soul-destroying experience.

Money and holiday time are also an issue. If you can only afford to go once a year, or find it difficult to get enough time off work, you probably want as good an experience as possible. Whereas someone who's retired and flying out to an event every weekend, may be willing to take bigger risks.

It's also a good idea to do some research ahead of time, about how the application process works. With some events, you literally just show up and pay for whatever milonga/workshops you want to do. There are usually variations on day and weekend passes, though be careful, because sometimes the "discount" means if you miss a single milonga, you'd have been better off paying for everything separately. Double-check you're getting what you think you're getting. I've known a "Festival Pass" that didn't include the last milonga. Other events will only let you book for the whole weekend and require you to do so well in advance.

Some have a vetting procedure, often including an Approved List of people that get the first refusal of places. If you're not on that List, it's not the end of the world, as there will most likely be places left over, but they may well make discrete enquiries about whether you're the sort of person they want.

You can help this process along, if you know people who are on the List to act as references. In essence, rather than the Organizer asking five random people if they know and like you, you pre-emptively point in them in the direction of people that (you hope) do. Bear in mind, if you're not on the approved list, in some Festivals, you're probably looking at being the FNG at the bottom of the totem pole and will be expected to put the hours in over a number of Events, before you get a decent number of the dances that you want (though obviously this is a very personal thing, so you may be happy with what you get.) Again, ask around among those who have been but aren't part of the in-crowd.

You're probably going to need to socialize and make nice too. This eventually leads to...

The After-Party

There's a certain sense of pride in surviving to the end. Some will celebrate it with a photo to be put on social media, with a tag about "The Survivors" or something similar. Others involve inordinate amounts of pizza. At its heart, it's a bonding experience, which can be pleasant in its own right and a good way to climb up the Totem Pole, so you're no longer the FNG next time.

The After-after Party

Want to know if you're really in with the In-crowd? There may well be another informal mini-milonga, after the after-party, probably at the house of someone who lives locally.

Gender balancing numbers and floors

I'm going to be somewhat cynical and suggest you treat claims of limited numbers and gender balancing with a pinch of salt. Yes, some events do manage to get them to work properly. But unfortunately at the time of writing, others just claim to, or will make a Big Deal about doing it one year and then quietly not do it the next.

The Organizers are laying down a lot of money to run this event. Realistically, it's thousands of dollars. They make their money back mostly through ticket sales. Simple as that. So there's a lot of incentive for them to have as many people as possible packed into the venue. I've turned up to a Festival to meet a friend who was just leaving, because he felt it had got so packed, that it was now a fire hazard. If someone knocked one of the table candles over, there was no way the people there were going to be able to exit safely and quickly. As I'd already pre-paid for the ticket, I went inside, had a look, danced one tanda and then decided he was right and went home.

Then there's the whole male/female approach to booking. Imagine the booking is opening on noon on the 1st of February. By one minute past noon, on the 1st of February, most of the women have booked. Three months later, halfway through the weekend of the event, the men start to consider whether they might like to go...

Ok, it's an exaggeration, but not by that much. Most men simply don't rush to book events in the same way that most women do. So now the Organizer has a problem. They announced prior to the booking opening, that this was going to be gender-balanced. Only now there's only a week to go before the event they've invested thousands of dollars in, and while they have two hundred women who have applied, so far, they only have twenty men.

What do they do? Stick to their guns and hope that the men get it together in time? Bear in mind, if they've only approved the first twenty women, then if they wait for the other hundred and eighty men to book, before confirming the corresponding women, those women who applied three months ago are going to be annoyed as they could have booked flights and accommodation a lot cheaper and closer to the venue, back then. Even if they do come, they're going to remember this next year, when deciding between returning here, or trying out their competition. (At the time of writing, there's usually at least one Tango Event every weekend of the year.) The local men, in particular, don't have to worry about hotels and planes. And in this example, the Organizer is running the risk of ending up with a grand total of forty people at their Event. Which if they needed two hundred, just break even, is a problem.

Or they could just let everyone come. They've got two hundred and twenty dancers, so they're going to make a profit anyway. Hopefully, enough men will turn up to balance things out...

There's also the middle ground, particularly if they have more experience as an Organizer. They can try to encourage some women to convince men to book with them, both to get themselves off the waiting list, and also both benefit from a slight discount by booking as a couple.

They can also make an educated guess on how many men will eventually book, based on experience. Let's say they think about a hundred and fifty will book by the end of the week. So they go ahead and confirm the first hundred and fifty women on the List. Great, that's now three hundred people coming, they've made a profit and are still gender-balanced. Well, as long as those predicted men all book.

Hopefully, you can see the flaws in all those plans. No-one wants to lose thousands of dollars if they can help it. But letting most of the women in and hoping the men will appear, can result in some fairly unbalanced situations. Especially as having "experience" as an Organizer is a bit of a misnomer when it comes to tango events. Organizing something once a year, for three years, does not make you "experienced", by any sane definition of the word. Dancers come and go, economies boom and recess, trends shift, your competition changes.

Ok, so what about numbers overall? In theory, the Fire Department puts an upper limit on how many people can be in any given venue. But given that they base this on everyone sitting down, the way the audience would for an orchestral concert, a tango event is never going to be that crowded. So it comes down to two problems.

Firstly, how crowded a floor is acceptable? Again bear in mind, the lower the number, the harder it's going to be to make a profit, unless you have a market that will pay extra for knowing there will be a reasonable amount of floorspace.

Secondly, the number of people dancing at any one time isn't a constant. At the beginning and end of an event, many people won't have arrived, or will have already left. Particularly with a marathon, the numbers are constantly in flux. And again, this is compounded by the problem of the men not deciding until the last minute.

So what does all that mean? Firstly, Organizers aren't really as Evil as people think. They're often trying to make the best of a chaotic situation, with limited information, whilst staking a considerable amount of money in the process. Secondly, you might want to consider having a back-up plan and an idea of what's acceptable to you. If you turn up to the Saturday night milonga and realize you're going to have to fight tooth and nail to get a dance, which will in turn involve you being pushed, shoved and kicked around on the dance floor, you might be better off going sight-seeing, or checking out the local theater instead.

Leaving your local area

When it going to events where you have to stay overnight, packing is an art form. Especially for women. Consider what will fold up into a small space and how you can mix and match clothes to get enough different looks for the weekend. Suitcase space is a premium, especially if you have to fly. Do an internet search to find out what the weather is going to be like to guide your choice of clothing, coats and so forth. If you're going to a different state or country, you might want to do some sightseeing, while you're there and what you're wearing to a milonga, may not be the most suitable attire.

Likewise, it pays to do some internet research on sightseeing ahead of time. Print off maps if that's how you mind works. Figure out what the opening and closing times are for places you want to visit and any likely fees. An internet search for "Student guide" and the city you're going to, can be surprisingly helpful. Also, figure out ahead of time how transportation works. Can you summon a taxi within minutes just using your phone, or do you need to get hold of grey market travel-cards just to get on a bus? In fact, can you use your phone as is, or do you need to sort out data roaming with your contractor, especially if you want to use it to navigate? Do you have the necessary chargers and adapters for whatever tech you can't live without?

Accommodation is largely a matter of budget and personal preference. Booking ahead of time will usually be significantly cheaper. Some hotels will let you cancel within a certain period without charging you a cancellation fee, which is useful if you're one of those unfortunate women on a waiting list. But make a note on your calendar, so you don't forget and end up getting charged if you can't go.

It's up to you if you want to stay in the same place as the majority of the other dancers. Some Festivals literally camp out in a venue, but it's not usually a problem if you want to go and stay in a nearby hotel and enjoy a comfy bed with room service, instead.

I'd advise you get hold of a stash of food when you arrive. It can be easy to lose track of time. Being able to grab a bar of chocolate, or eat a banana can help tide you over, either to keep on dancing, or to revive you enough to get you somewhere that will serve you a proper meal. Taking some time to scope out where the places are that serve food you like, especially those open late at night, or early on a Sunday morning, can also help a lot.

Chapter 13 – Here be Dragons

"How do beginners get better, if no-one better than them will dance
with them?"

~ Ghost

Social media can be a very effective tool for getting dances. You can message people ahead of time to check they're going and even "book" dances with them. It can be a useful source of information about cities you're planning on visiting and the local milongas there. People who like your posts, but who have never met you, will usually be happy to dance with you and can often get you introduced to other local dancers. You can also raise your profile by posting pictures of yourself at events, or wandering around Buenos Aires.

"I'm nearly finished packing for Buenos Aires!!!"

"In that case I look forward to endless pictures on FB and you mentioning it every second sentence when you come back"

"I'm not sure if I can be restrained enough for only saying it every second sentence. I mean it's Buenos Aires after all"

"Good point. Well then I'll look forward to your triumphant return as a dramatically better dancer"

"Yeah, because that always happens to the people who go there"

"I think there's a ceremony. Involving angel tears or something..."

"Haha. Well it will raise my tango profile, that's for sure. Be interesting to see who wants to dance me when I come back, that wouldn't before."

"And in fairness, being in a very different place to normal, things may well click, you might get new insights."

"Yeah, I remember last time. I found it an incredible loco place, nothing at all like home - nothing works, it's definitely not a 1ˢᵗ World city. So much is just broken and yet it somehow careens along in its own wild way. And the dancing is something else."

"Don't forget the shoes!"

The Fickleness of the "Going" category

For some reason, when it comes to Events that are publicized on social media, people have always been fickle about the "Going" button. I remember being told by someone, before social media even existed, that they used to organize Business Events that had tickets costing hundreds of dollars. And yet people would book, pay for the ticket and not turn up. To be clear, this wasn't they had an emergency and rang up to cancel, or ask for a partial refund. They just simply didn't turn up.

So I would strongly advise you don't make any Big Decisions about going to an Event based on the "Going" section.

You may read, or write on online groups, forums, or indeed blogs. A well written blog can raise your profile and get you more dances. But, frankly unless you really enjoy writing and random abuse from strangers, it's a lot of work and there are easier ways.

Which leads us to Forums and social media. Online discussions should probably come with mental health warnings. They're often a lot like car crashes. You don't want to look, but... Well, actually it can be surprisingly similar. Scientists now think the reason we look at car crashes isn't because we're all sick and twisted, it's because we're seeing if there's anything we need to learn from the situation, to prevent it happening to us.

The reason this book exists is that dancers don't really have these conversations. Surely a serious online discussion group would solve that? Um, no. There's usually the odd diamond in the rough, if you're willing to hang in there, but it's almost always a terrible return on your time for anything other than killing time when you should be working. And in the process, you'll be fed an awful lot of "facts" that are nothing more than half-assed opinions.

You'll also discover, in no uncertain terms, that not everyone who dances Argentine Tango is a nice person, which can be a bit disheartening.

Words have consequences

There's a lot of important things it's easy to forget, or even simply not realize, when dealing with social media. One of the main ones is that not everyone thinks the same way you do. The four types model I've used throughout this book, is the tip of the Iceberg. Myers Briggs, Belbin, Jung, there's a lot of different ways to look at the world. But with a big enough group of people, no matter what you say, you'll find some who agree with you. Even if you advocate murdering kittens.

And that can be a problem. Let's say you post that the cabeceo is Evil. And three people agree with you. There's a lot of likes and by the time you've finished the discussion, you've somehow moved from them being Evil, to "Anyone who does the cabeceo really shouldn't have any rights at all." There may a few people who try to slow down this train wreck, but they'll often jump off when they see it's built up too much steam. There may also be a few people who try to be polite about it because they don't want to get into an online fight with the Crazy

People. (That would be you in this case.)

"But I enjoy the free-for-all banter."

Before you get too carried away, bear in mind that usually only a small percentage of the people who are reading, actually post comments. It's quite possible for you to post something and have everyone else who posts agree with you, while the people who you want to dance with socially, read it, don't post anything and promptly put you on their "Do not dance with the Crazy Person" list.

Get far enough out of hand, and the thread will get copied and pasted. So even if you thought you were posting to a limited forum on a Closed Group, that genie is now out of his bottle and isn't going back in. You know those pictures of elementary school teachers holding up a piece of paper asking you to share it, so their students can see how far something can travel around the internet? That effect is now happening to you, and it's not limited to the internet. People can talk about it in the Real World too.

All of that can cost you dances.

"I love you, I hate you!"

People also change over time. There's a lot of reasons for this. Relationships end, some have an epiphany and want to change styles, or they might reach a point where they either "get" your dancing or stop "getting" it and want something else. They may have their own imaginary league tables in their heads, or convoluted equations of Correct Behavior. They may simply have been misinformed or misunderstood your actions, or indeed inactions. In short, understanding and exploring the social dynamics of tango could keep psychologists employed for decades.

My best advice is to try not to take it too seriously, or indeed too personally. It can seem Very Real when everyone is hugging at the end of a Festival and social media is filled with tagged photos of everyone saying how Incredible and Life-Changing dancing with you is. But it's mostly well-intentioned smoke and mirrors. The lights come back on, everyone changes into their jeans and they go back to work and their everyday lives. And so it fades.

If you look on social media, you'll see a lot of people who do tango, tend to have a very high proportion of tango friends. In the short term, non-tango friends will often give you some leeway when it comes to meeting up. So if they're going to a bar and you decide to go to a milonga instead, but then find it's rubbish, you can leave and go and meet your friends at the bar. Mobile phones are great for this. If you eventually leave tango, or end up in a situation where you need people you can depend on, that's when you'll be glad you missed some of those milongas and maintained your friendships outside of tango.

Or worse, someone has a Tango Fight with someone else. Some will pick sides. Some sit on the fence. Others sit back and throw popcorn. And suddenly you realize how incredibly fickle it can all be. I've seen entire milongas suddenly shift and alienate anyone there who wasn't of the "correct" style. I've seen people looking around, wondering where all their "friends" who said they were wonderful, had suddenly disappeared to, now that they actually needed some support?

This is another good reason not to neglect your non-tango friends. No matter who breaks up with who in the tango world, your friends outside tango will still be there for you, and unless you somehow managed to murder some actual kittens in the process, they'll generally assume you're in the right and won't care less what anyone from tango is saying about you, other than to be annoyed on your behalf. As one friend delicately put it, "Who the ******* **** do they think they are?!"

On being turned down, it happens

Hopefully after just reading that catastrophe of how bad things can get, being turned down for a dance no longer seems quite as bad? Again, most of tango is just smoke and mirrors. Yes, you can make some good friendships, but on the whole, people tend to overstate the importance, of, well, almost everything in tango. No-one in any milonga is rejecting *You*. How could they? Who in this milonga actually knows who you are in any real depth? Sure, they know what you had for breakfast, because you felt compelled to put it on social media, but what about your real hopes and dreams, the rich tapestry that makes you a complete, unique person? Yeah, they've no clue.

Most of the time they aren't even rejecting the version of you they've hastily created in their mind. And I do mean hastily. How informed a decision can someone really hope to make in two seconds? There's a reason job interview take ages, and they still make terrible choices a lot of the time. Have you ever had to fill out a detailed questionnaire for anyone, before they'd dance tango with you?

But like I say, most of the time, it's Other Stuff. They're in a bad mood, they're injured, blah blah, woof woof. It really doesn't matter. People are people. And that encompasses a lot of weird and wonderful reasons for doing things that you'll probably never consider in your lifetime. You might want to re-read that last sentence and let it sink in. I know someone who will dance with anyone wearing a Dr Who t-shirt.

There's one more level to it. Most of the time, all that just happened was they turned down this tanda with you. That's it. Or rather, they turned down what they *think* this tanda would be like with their cut-out cardboard version of you. They did not turn down every dance with you for the end of time. They didn't even turn down every dance for this evening. But sometimes, even that didn't happen. They were just zoned out, or concentrating on something else. They didn't even turn you down. It was just they either didn't notice you at all, or by the time they registered you were there, you'd given up and moved on. Which again, has nothing to do with you.

So, yeah, stop thinking that if someone doesn't accept your invitation you deserve to have your Spirit crushed. You really don't.

The Ice experiment

One of the stranger ways your memory plays tricks is regarding pain. An experiment was carried out involving putting people's arms in ice water. (Psychologists have come up with some pretty dark experiments over the years!) The people in the first group were allowed to remove their arm at the ten minute mark. The members of the second group had to keep their arm in the ice water for twenty minutes, but for the last ten minutes, the water was gradually heated back to room temperature.

Both groups were asked to evaluate the "unpleasantness" of the experience. Surprisingly, the group that had their arms in ice water for only ten minutes, rated it as much more unpleasant than the second group. What this means in tango, is if you have a bad experience in a milonga and you leave immediately, you'll remember it as being much worse than if you stayed a bit, had a mediocre tanda and then left. Which in turn, will also affect how you feel during your journey home.

"Frog in a blender"

A follower I know, coined this delightful phrase to describe the experience of dancing with certain leaders. It turns out there's two versions, the physical one she was describing, and the emotional one where the leader explains to you in excruciating detail, how everything you're doing is wrong, leaving you a wreck. And in the spirit of equality, there are followers who will inflict both versions on leaders too.

The only time I've ever known this "feedback" to be accurate information is where pain was involved. It's possible to cause a surprising amount of pain to the person you're dancing with and not realize. But among the dancers who actually know what they're doing, 99% of the time, they'll either suffer in silence, or simply say, "Would you mind adjusting your embrace like this?" It definitely won't feel like an endless lecture on why you are an awful dancer.

If someone is giving you what feels like a soul-destroying critique of your dance, they almost certainly have no clue what they're talking about. You'll see them from time to time at lessons, prácticas and milongas, trying to get it "right" by following the instructions from another Workshop, or the Correct Method espoused by a Maestro, or often from their interpretation of what they think is right based on an online video clip... They often have a fixed partner, who will be trying to desperately gain the power of telepathy in the absence of any consistent or accurate connection, whilst being constantly "corrected".

So what do you do? Well, first of all understand, IT'S NOT YOUR FAULT. Yes, you probably think this person is an "advanced dancer" and knows what they're talking about, but this kind of behavior is the tango equivalent of boasting about your new Rolaax watch (*Available from the street dealer of your choice. Looks almost like the real thing! Batteries not included. May cause allergic reactions.*)

Secondly, whichever version you've had the misfortune to encounter, go and find the gentlest, kindest person you know and tell them, in no more than one sentence, that you've just been through hell and would really appreciate a gentle dance to help get over the experience. You're in a room with people and no matter which part of the Competitive/Nurturing/Free Spirit/Cooperative spectrum you are, some of them will be happy to give you hugs and agree with you that the person was a Jerk (though for remarkably different reasons.) This should help convert your stress into some nice, warm, oxytocin fuzzies, for both of you.

Which leads to another of tango's Big Questions.

Walking away from a tanda

There should be suitably dramatic music at this point! Most of what you believe about this is sensible, logical and wrong. Unfortunately, it means you probably make bad decisions.

As I explained in Chapter 8, if you want to politely end a tanda early, simply say, "Thank-you." This is code for "we're finished dancing now." Saying "Thank-you" at the end of a tanda, just means "thank-you."

There's no hidden meaning in this case.

Here's a simple idea that you will immediately go, "Yes, but..." to. That's ok. Everyone does.

Argentine Tango is a social dance. Despite the frankly, depressing music and the soul-destroying online discussion, it is supposed to be something you enjoy. So it makes sense that the aim of dancing socially, should on some level, be about enjoyment. Or at least getting more experience to get better, so you can enjoy it more. There are some dances when this just isn't happening. Sometimes it can be Frog in a Blender territory, but, and this is important, sometimes it's no-one's fault at all.

Take a moment to think about that, because no-one ever really talks about it.

There's a lot of different ways to dance. Soft, energetic, lyrical, crazy, serene, full-on, and that's even before you look at the different styles, teaching methods, body types... Now add in the different moods you can be in throughout an evening. Whether you're warmed-up? What the DJ is doing with the music? There's a lot of reasons why the two of you may simply not be on the same page for this particular tanda.

Rather than carrying on and suffering through this train wreck, you can stop, politely thank each other and then each find someone else who is on your page, so all four of you can enjoy what remains of this tanda.

Unless things are truly awful, most people will wait until the end of the first song to say "thank-you." It gives both of you a chance to sync up. However, if it's clear that this just isn't going to work, it's better to just stop and say "thank-you". You'll most likely get a look of relief from the other person. Rather than suffer through the rest of the dance, you have the option to either invite someone else immediately, or take the rest of the dance to mentally catch your breath and then ask someone.

And then, if you want, the two of you can try another tanda later on, when things have shifted again and you're hopefully both on the same page again.

Put like that it seems an easy choice. But often, everyone focuses on blame. It must be someone's Fault and there must be Consequences.

Why?

Now there may be exceptions to this who I haven't met, but I'll let you into a secret. The people who will blacklist you if you end a tanda early. The ones who proclaim how such dancers should be publicly stoned. The ones who make you think that it's better to suffer for fifteen minutes with them than to walk away. All of those that I've known are **terrible** dancers. Not just bad. Terrible. As a more experienced follower eloquently put it.

"I hate these guys! They should be banned... shot in the feet."

So getting on their blacklist is actually a good thing. They tend to rely on dancing with people who are frightened of the Consequences and who are inexperienced enough to mistake being "more advanced than them" as "good", rather than recognize just how awful they are. Like the Great and Powerful Oz they put on a good show, as long as you don't look behind the curtain. They'll make a point of saying "Hi" to the teachers/organizers/DJ. They'll probably have been dancing for years and they'll be happy to regale you of their trip to Buenos Aires and other exotic lands. They may even know who Podestá *(po-deh-STAH – a famous tango singer)* is. In the words of another experienced follower

"Mr. Paid-for-private-lessons with Horacio Godoy and Chicho Frumboli. Now there is no reason why this fellow shouldn't be a nice dancer but the 'been there, paid for this, read that' approach is hardly going to work as a wow-factor if he has little to show for it right here, right now, with me...Unwowed."

Sadly, I could fill up pages with similar heartfelt quotes about this.

Bottom line. You have total permission to politely walk away from any tanda, at any point, and to say, "No" whenever you want.

When it all goes wrong

Doc Eason passed on a useful piece of information which I'll paraphrase here.

"When people tell you that you're a great dancer, don't believe them. There's a lot of reasons they might be saying this. They might honestly believe it, but have no clue what 'good' actually is. They might be trying to be polite, to save your feelings, or even to usher you away. Take all those compliments and accept them graciously, but then fold them up and put them away in your back pocket.

Then one night, it will happen. You will find yourself at the end of the evening, completely demoralized. Things will have gone horribly. You will know with Utter Certainty that you are Rubbish and should quit. It will probably be raining.

When that fateful night comes, reach into your back pocket and pull out the time that someone looked at you with big eyes and told you were the Best Dancer Ever!"

I would add, that you should probably go and eat some chocolate and generally pamper yourself.

Chapter 14 - How to enter the Milonga, where Pixie Dust is free

I'm shattered, sitting down after a whirlwind milonga with a dervish and trying to remember to slowly sip the water, rather than follow my instinct to gulp. My friend comes over to me. She looks a bit dazed and she has big, wide anime eyes. There's a softness to her whole energy and the way she's moving that I don't often see.

"That was amazing..."

How do you get to experience this, every dance, night after night?

This was by far the hardest chapter to write. It drifts in and out of being "Woo", though there's solid science that underpins a lot of the "why". It's a reflection of society that the people who talk about this stuff tend to be the shamen, the holy men and women of the tribe, the poets, storytellers and indeed the dancers, and the language used reflects that. Fortunately there are also mad scientists who've put enthusiastic, meditating Buddhist monks into CAT Scanners, to try to decipher these mysteries in the more concrete terms of electrons and neurons. If you're into Woo, then you'll enjoy this chapter. Feel free to get some Herbal Tea, or a glass of wine.

If you're not into Woo, I'd strongly recommend you read it anyway, especially to the end. Try to translate it into terms that make sense to you. It really doesn't matter whether it's your hippocampus working at a certain frequency, to a blend of oxytocin and adrenaline, or "pixie dust". This is the chapter that can transform your tango. So if you want to get a drink and mutter as you read the "Hippie nonsense", go for it.

Process vs outcome

Are you looking to enjoy "The journey", or are you more focused on achievements and the destination? For some people, this is just obvious. They go dancing to have a good time and are especially happy when they have a "moment", whether that's a great dance, or catching up with a good friend over a glass of wine all night. Or they get a buzz from achieving "something". Maybe they want to learn all the moves, or be admired by their peers, or get a dance with "that person".

There's nothing wrong with either of those approaches. I do however, offer a word of caution if you're focussed on a destination. When you get there, it may turn out to look rather different to what you imagined.

In the changing world of tango, when you get there, it may even turn out that it no longer exists. There are plenty of tango dancers who have never even heard of Carlos Gavito, let alone know how to dance in his style. I know a lot of frustrated people who got where they wanted to be in tango, looked around and realized there was no-one they wanted to dance with, and nowhere they wanted to dance! It wouldn't have been quite so bad if they're at least enjoyed the journey there. But because they kept telling themselves "I'll be happy when..." they ended up just spending a lot of time and money making themselves miserable for years.

Tango is one of those hobbies that you can enjoy from day one. Role-players sometimes talk about the Golden Zone. This is the idea that to really enjoy playing a certain character, or computer game, you first need to get to a certain point. And then it's great! Until you reach the end of the Golden Zone at which point it stops being enjoyable.

It's in your own interest to have as big a Golden Zone as possible in Tango. In particular, be wary of any plan that basically involves a lifetime of misery and you being happy for one perfect day before you die. While this may seem like heresy, keep in mind that tango was extinct for decades. Just because it exists now, is no guarantee it'll be around in ten, or even five years time. If you're buying into the idea that it'll take you ten years to get to the point where you can enjoy yourself, that may be a problem.

If you've ever gone home after a milonga asking yourself "Why?"

The silver lining is that this often happens, just before you have a revelation that makes your dancing better. I don't know why it works this way, but it's something that's been reported across cultures for a long time and has many names. Two days ago, on November 6th, 2016, Stephen Curry missed all ten of the three-point shots he took and his team, the Golden State Warriors, lost by twenty points. If you don't play basketball, just know that's about as bad as it gets for a professional player. Tonight, in a game against the New Orleans Pelicans, he successfully made **thirteen**, three-point shots, breaking the existing record! Oh and his team also won. So if you've had a bad night, don't give up. You might be in for a treat.

On the other hand, it's possible you've outstayed your welcome at this particular venue. Places change slowly over time. It's possible that the milonga that you enjoyed dancing in six months ago, has changed enough so that it's no longer a place you enjoy any more. Maybe the people you liked have left. Maybe the organizer is trying something new. Maybe there's a new DJ, or a new fashion that rubs you up the wrong way. In which case, it's probably time to think about trying somewhere new, or having a break for a while.

It might also just be a part of the natural progression of being a social tango dancer. It's not at all unusual for someone to start off hesitant, then go through a "mad" phase of dancing as many nights a week as possible! But eventually that, too, passes and you find yourself wanting something else and dancing less because of it. It's a bit like you've been given the keys to the sweetshop. At first, you're not sure how things work. Is this some kind of test to see if you're honest and won't eat all the sweets? But then you realize you can eat all the sweets! Woo hoo! Eventually you find yourself sitting on the floor surrounded by sweet wrappers and you realize that all you really want is a nice, cool glass of water. Unfortunately no-one seems to know where you can get one. Some people find the phase that suits them and stay there. Others keep cycling through, going back to the beginning every few years.

The biggest problem with this piece of advice is that people simply won't believe you. Tell the skittish beginner that there will come a time when they'll be dancing six nights a week and regularly jetting off to dance around Europe, and they'll look at you like a character from the beginning of a children's film "No, not me. Someone else, surely?" Tell the person who's dancing six nights a week that eventually they'll tire of this, and they will also treat you as if you are completely mad. It's just seems to be something people have to live through in their own way and in their own time.

Looking and being seen

This causes a lot of confusion. It's easy to jump to conclusions about how it works, but it's pretty much a matter of Woo (or building subconscious heuristics, if you prefer.) Let's break it down.

Some people want to be looked at. It's easy to jump to the example of the stereotypical, "nuevo chick", dressed like a stripper and moving like a pole dancer, but it's not necessarily the case. It could just as easily be the person looking like a librarian who really wants people to look at their elegant footwork. Likewise, the aforementioned pole dancer might just be enjoying a night of dressing up and having fun, with no thought about who looks at them.

Wanting to be seen has a distinct vibe. Some people call it "pulling light". If there were a spotlight in the milonga, it would be on them, whether they're dancing or sitting. This can be really confusing when it comes to asking for dances. You can feel they want you to look at them. If you're particularly empathic, it will feel almost magnetic. But just because they want you to look at them, doesn't mean they want to look at you. When they don't, it feels like the invitation has got stuck in a loop. You can feel them wanting you to look at them. So you look at them. But they don't look back at you. And so you wonder what you're doing wrong? Instead, stop and ask yourself "Do they want to look at me?"

Some people don't want to be looked at. They're the ninja of the milonga. But that doesn't mean they don't want to dance with you. So now you experience the reverse situation. Someone who is clearly trying to avoid people looking at them, but who is over-joyed if you ask them to dance. Again, there's a vibe of "Let it be me! Please pick me!" mixed in with "Don'tletanyoneseeme." It mostly feels like someone is really shy. It often lacks the confidence of someone brazenly enjoying knowing that you're looking at them and they're not going to look back at you. However, the master ninja, will somehow appear to be invisible to everyone else, while smiling invitingly at you.

Another version of this can be truly heart-wrenching. Someone who's been sitting out for so long, with no hope of it getting better, that they start putting the clothing they arrived in, back on. And you would think that it would be compassionate to go and ask them for a dance. Sometimes they don't want to be saved, or more specifically, they don't want to be saved by you. Again, ask yourself, does this person want to see me?

Tango as a Religious Experience

William James writes about the many ways humans have religious experiences in his book, Varieties of Religious Experience. Turns out that tango can indeed tick all the boxes of a religious experience. William James makes a lot of useful points. His premise is that the "religious experience" is fundamentally the same, regardless of the actual religion, culture, period in history and so on. This particularly applies to tango when people start to follow The One True Way.

The One True Way in tango, is when a person has found what works for them, here and now. Sometimes it's just a matter of luck. They started with a teacher and venue that suits them. Often there's some kind of Authority involved, such as "My teacher's, teacher, is from Buenos Aires" or "This style is a genuine Buenos Aires style." But it can also come about through conversion.

They begin with a certain style, or indeed get to the "dancing six nights a week" stage, and then realize something is lacking. They find themselves on the floor of the sweetshop and suddenly realize that all they really want is a glass of water! This is often cheerfully called the Dark Night of the Soul. And again, it's surprisingly popular in myths and their modern-day equivalent, film. Let's kill off your loved ones and leave you abandoned and powerless, so that you can have a story arc and overcome the odds, proving that you are indeed worthy of living happily ever after.

I'm not entirely kidding about killing off your loved ones either. In the "sweet shop" phase, it can be very easy to feel that you simply do not have time for your family and non-tango friends. I've known people who had friends visiting from another continent and they took them out "for a drink", to a milonga, where they danced, a lot, while their friends sat there.

It's also why some people will continue to dance when injured or ill. The idea of taking a week or two off to heal and get better, seems insane to them.

It's long been observed that people who have given up cigarettes for good, tend to be far more extreme about the evils of smoking, than those who never smoked in the first place. This also happens in tango. Someone starts off in open embrace, experiences their Dark Night of the Soul and finds close embrace. You would think this is a good thing. And for some it is. But for others they turn into Prophets for their Cause.

This is where it gets a bit confusing, understanding which kind of zealot you're dealing with. Is it someone who's just accepted what they were told from the get-go and has been told that all unbelievers are either nuts, or need to be converted? Or is this someone who lost their faith and having rediscovered it, is again out to either convert, or dismiss anyone who disagrees with them?

In case you think I'm inferring too much calling Tango a religious experience, take a moment and ask yourself, how much time does an average Hindu, Christian, Jew, Moslem, Wiccan etc, spend praying each week? Roughly. Not the really devoted ones, the average ones who turn up to their place of worship once or twice a year and for special occasions, like marriage and funerals. How much money do they spend on their religion? Maybe $5 or $10 in donations a year, if that.

Now ask yourself those same questions about the more devoted tango dancers. How much time and money do they spend practising, going to lessons and milongas, talking about tango, buying shoes and clothes, taking private lessons, going to Festivals. Let's face it, Buenos Aires has become tango's Mecca, Jerusalem, or Rome.

"But there's no deity in Tango!" True, though it's telling that we often refer to the best dancers as gods and goddesses. Still, it's important to make the distinction between tango as a religion (it's not) and tango as a religious *experience*, which it can be. This is useful to know if you, or the surrounding people, are experiencing it this way. You can fly very high in tango and like Icarus, you can fall from a great height too.

You may find yourself the lone voice, trying to convince everyone else that they should convert to nuevo, or the cabeceo, or close embrace. It will sound reasonable to you! But if you find yourself feeling frustrated that no-one seems to be listening, well, next time the Jehovah's Witnesses turn up at your door, perhaps be a bit more understanding.

"That was amazing..."

If you say this to someone about a dance you just had with someone else, the most likely response is going to be "Why?" While I totally understand that smiling a lot and saying "I don't know, it just was!" makes perfect sense to you, bear in mind, if you're talking to someone who dances the opposite role to you, it maybe frustrating to them, especially if they're trying to infer what would make them a better dancer. You're probably better off making these kinds of statements to people who have the same role as you, or dancers with enough experience to already know the answer.

Now we come to the last elusive part. The final piece of the puzzle. I've saved this for last because once you understand it, milongas will never be the same for you again. In fact, after you've read this part, I encourage you to think back over the rest of the book, in light of this.

How do you consistently get "That was amazing" experiences, not just every once in a while, but every dance, night after night?

Think back to when you woke up this morning. You got up at a certain time, got out of the same side of bed you always do. You brushed your teeth, sorted out your hair, just as you did yesterday. You even put your socks, or tights, on the same foot first, the same way you've been doing for years. And so the day continues. Most people do things a certain way, especially at work, or school. We get into ruts and habits and even the chaotic Free Spirits, tend to find themselves living in a world of organized people. Or looked at another way, humans naturally build tiny rituals into everything they do. We even talk about getting out of the wrong side of bed.

The Milonga is an escape for this. A place of fantasy. Where you can dress up as a princess, or express your more sensual, or artistic side. Where you can leave behind your day job as a manual worker, don a suit and be the dashing anti-hero of the play. Or drive up in a BMW, wearing shoes that cost a year's wage for someone in the 1920s and dance "authentically" to music from Tango's "Golden Age" (played on someone's laptop.)

Archaic codes and rituals, replace those of which sock to put on first. As music fills the room, the two Angels may appear, singing arcane lyrics of love and despair, only to then vanish in a cloud of feathery notes. Mix in a dash of alcohol and a soupçon of oxytocin, dopamine, serotonin and adrenalin, and you can enter another world, where all the men and women are merely players, with their entrances and exits.

Just like in every good fairytale, the normal rules don't quite work here. You're not in Kansas any-more. Unlike Dorothy, you can choose to hop between stories. If this one isn't quite to your liking (for example, you don't want to dance with Flying Monkeys), you can go and find another one that is. Trying to explain to the Wicked Witch that she's just misunderstood and she really should dance with you, rather than trying to kill your puppy, is rarely a good plan. Don't fall into the trap of thinking that the way things normally work is how they should work here. The Friar doesn't get to make-out with Juliet. Romeo doesn't get a happy ending.

The Milonga is Mardi Gras, it's the Circus. It's Catholic Benediction and Ecstatic Dervishes, all rolled up into one. Hot dogs become Empenadas. The tangy blend of aftershave, perfumes, talc and sweat, is our exotic, burning incense. DJ technomancers work their arts on laptops, bringing tandas that make you soar and fall, speaking of love and loss and tragedy. Candles, both real and electric, flicker on tables, sending shadows flitting around the hall. Time starts to bend and shift. Moments for the dancers, stretch out for an eternity to those who wait outside the ronda.

"Your soul is a seeker, lover and artist; shape-shifting through archetypal energy, between your darkness and fields of light, your body and spirit, your heaven and hell, until you land in the moment of sweet surrender; when you, as a dancer, disappear into the dance." ~ *Gabrielle Roth*

The Points System

That's all very poetic, but what does it actually mean? Many view their time at a milonga as a kind of points system, where each dance gets or loses you a certain number of points depending on how it goes. At the end of the night, you add up all the points and that's how well it went. You can also add points for talking to people, if you enjoyed that. Oh and buying shoes.

Some women are referred to as "La Planchadora" *(la plan-cha-DOR-ah - A woman who sits all night at the milonga without being asked to dance.)* Clearly they lose each time, because they don't amass a significant amount of points. The problem is, this description misses out a rather important piece of information. How does she feel about this? There are men and women who go to a milonga simply to meet up with friends and spend the evening chatting over drinks. There are those who impishly sit with their legs curled up as they sketch the dancers. These people aren't miserable.

And then there are those who dance every tanda, but one, and are miserable for that one tanda.

Let's take a look at La Planchadora's twin sister. She also spends most of the night sitting out alone. But for some reason, she seems happy, even serene about it. Presumably she's just deluded, right?

No, she knows the last secret of the Milonga and it's one that changes everything.

Take two guys. One is walking down Bourbon Street. He's got his earphones in and his music is blaring away. He's staring at his phone as he pecks out a message with his finger. He occasionally mutters to himself that it's too hot and crowded.

The other guy is about five feet away from him, in slacks and a shirt. His collar's undone and he's leaning back easily against the wall. He's taking in his surroundings and there's an almost childlike light in his eyes.

Despite they're both being in the same place, only one of them is actually in Mardi Gras.

To the confusion of beginners, "milonga" already has two meanings, the place and a style of music. I'm going to add a third, with a capital "M".

Entering the Milonga

The Milonga isn't the physical space. It's a state of mind. There's a lot that goes on in a Milonga, that comes from religious practices, the theater, the Circus, even advertising. If you'll let it, it changes your state of mind, putting you in a trance. But in doing so, it gives you access to bountiful energy. If you're in a milonga and you're pining over the dances you're not getting, or complaining about the floorcraft, or a million other things, then you're not in the Milonga. Not yet.

So how do you enter?

First relax. This isn't something you try to do. You're just going to let it happen. Use all your senses.

Look around.

Focus on the candles. Look at them flickering. There's something primal about watching fire. Breathe in the air, smell the perfumes and aftershaves, mixed with the bitter tang of coffee and sweat, tango's own blend of incense. Look at the shadows playing across the floor, walls and ceilings, something humans have been doing since we were in caves.

Let your gaze roam and discover the liquids in the various glasses and jugs. See how they manipulate and reflect the light. Watch how the wine changes its shape as the glass is lifted. Look at the shiny things, the glasses and metals. Listen to the beat of the music. Different rhythms can have a deep effect on your brain. Watch the expressions on the dancers' faces, rapture, childish delight, profound seriousness, and your subconscious will start to react. Don't wear a watch, let yourself lose track of time (unless you need to catch a train!)

The beauty of it is you don't need to do anything. You don't need to chant, or rotate your chakras. It doesn't matter whether Mercury is in retrograde. Just become aware of these things and your brain is hard-wired to take care of the rest.

Let it.

It's a lot like falling asleep. You don't really "try" to fall asleep, you just wake up the next morning and realize you did. Dancers and shamen and dancing shamen, have been doing this forever. Duende, nagual, zazen, mushin, the Silver Desert, Dreamtime, the Eternal Now. They didn't need online videos, or even electricity.

Entering the Milonga is like waking up and knowing you're still dreaming. For each person, the experience is slightly different. For me, it's as if everything is being shot by an artsy photographer. I see a softly lit shoe, casting a portentous shadow across a wooden floor, when all I'm doing is tying my laces. You might feel somber, or mischievous. It's something you just have to experience.

But once you're finally in the Milonga, it fills you up with its energy. Forget about starting from zero and trying to claw your way up in some strange game of snakes and ladders. You've already won. That's why the woman is sitting there with that knowing smile on her face. She's filled to the brim with joy. If anything, she's trying not to show it, lest you think her mad.

Whereas before the crowded floor, with it's bumping and inconsiderate floorcraft, either aggravated you, or inspired you to battle, now you just see it as part of the Milonga, no different from a heaving Mosh Pit, standing room only at a Concert, or the Vatican Basilica at Easter. It adds to the energy. Rather than shying away from it, embrace it, let it bring you more deeply into the Milonga. You find you're no longer saying "Sorry" over missed leads.

You're no longer worried about dancing the same four moves over and over, or how pretty your adornments are. Because on a primal level you're Inspired. You're transported to Mardi Gras, partnered with Angels, Harlequins and Mysterious Strangers. Lose yourself in a sense of wonder and enjoy the party. Let that feeling of inspiration permeate your dancing, so that your partner becomes a part of it.

The four types model also shifts. Outside of the Milonga, they can often feel adversarial. But in it, you realize they're just different instruments of a band, or ingredients in a good gumbo. It shifts from being about them and us, to something greater.

We tend to see ourselves as more complex and nuanced (and usually well intentioned) while we can sometimes see others as less so, and we categorize their behavior more easily. And additionally, how we interpret the behavior of others and how we treat them in light of this, in turn, has an impact on how they behave.

Take the "haughty entitled vixens" for example. They dressed up and drove all that way, paid all that money and faced just as much uncertainty about the evening ahead as anyone else. But if no one greets them warmly, or makes a little conversation, because they're thinking, "Oh here's that stuck up, competitive madam again" then that can become their assigned role and the prophecy continues to fulfil itself.

Rather than rigidly reinforcing the categories, embrace the energy of the Milonga and rise above it. Be generous in your interpretations, and give yourself and others the freedom to move beyond a set of behaviors.

Each dancer brings something unique to the Milonga. In spite of everything else going on in our lives, this is something we can make a conscious decision about. Deciding to be positive and allow yourself to be in the moment, makes for a better experience for you and those around you. Come in a negative, or calculating frame of mind and it will create quite the opposite. The Dark Arts aren't needed here.

Find where you feel your energy. For some it's the base of their spine, others, their abdomen, heart, or crown of their head. Wherever it is, lift from it. Perhaps because of the music, perhaps there is someone you want to dance with, or simply because you have managed to get away from everything else in your life for a few hours. And if none of that works - lift your energy anyway!

This is also the last missing element to inviting someone to dance. When you invite someone else who is in the Milonga, it's a completely different experience. You share the moment together and it's beautiful. Time stretches and there's no rush or jitteryness.

Sadly, it's become a rare thing in today's world to be able to look someone in the eye for more than a few seconds. Savor this moment. Even if you go all the way over and they say "No", when you're in the Milonga, it will still feel like a positive experience.

Conversely, when you're not there, the invitation can be a frustrating, confusing mess that leaves you feeling battered and bruised inside.

It takes time to get into the Milonga, for many people, often hours, if at all. Which is why many will drink alcohol to speed things up. The problem is that often it only takes a moment to knock them back out again. Then they don't manage to get back in, before they have to go home. I went through a period of having incredible dances with a friend halfway through the evening and then someone would turn up later on and upset her and boom, that would be it until the next time I saw her. How fast you can get into the Milonga is also a matter of practice. Some people already know how to do something similar. Maybe they meditate, or they just really like hugging people.

Many never enter the Milonga at all. Or, now and then, they do so for a single tanda. There are times when you enter the Milonga and you realize that no-one has, or is going to. If you've found yourself wondering why you had a great dance with someone last time, but this time it was off, or they wouldn't even dance with you this week, one of you may not be in the Milonga right now.

An upside of this is the invitation can tell you how deeply in the Milonga they are. If it's a clunky confused mess, or you feel worse afterwards, then that wasn't go to be The Dance, no matter how much you adore them, or how great if was last time. It does mean that it's worth trying again later.

Taking the approach that if someone doesn't accept your invitation, you won't dance with them that night is counter-productive.

If you had a great dance with someone and were then terrified of asking them for another tanda "in case it wasn't as good", you managed to knock yourself out of the Milonga. The answer is to get back in and when you do, it'll just seem obvious that you should dance some more with them and it will be wonderful.

In case you need more convincing, ask yourself which of these two people are going to get more of the amazing dances they want?

You saw him enter a few minutes ago, visibly still angry from his experience of the city's traffic. There's already an empty glass on the table in front of him. He knows he's starting at zero. Who here can offer him some points that will, maybe, start to make this night worthwhile after all? As soon as the cortina starts, he begins stalking around the room, his shoulders still high and tensed in the after-image of his fury, his arms folded across his chest, growing tighter and tighter in desperation, as the woman after woman suddenly find their handbags fascinating...

- - -

You didn't see her arrive. You just realized she was there, somehow. There's a look on her face, of almost beatific, inner peace, yet even from here, you can see there's a glint of mischief twinkling in her eyes. The cortina is playing and she's looking around as if she's seeing something more than everyone else. Her fingertips are softly circling the top of her glass in time to the music. She waits until the tanda starts, cocking her head slightly to savor it and the glint of mischief starts to spread across her face in a grin...

The Book of Woo

Go and play with these ideas. Look back over the time you've spent in milongas and recognize when you caught glimpses of the Milonga, saw other people in it, or spent time in it yourself. Go to actual milongas and try it out. Like your first tango steps, it may be a bit uncertain at first. That's ok. As you start to get the hang of it, go back to the very beginning of this book and re-read it through the lens of the Milonga. You'll find a second, far more advanced book, hidden in plain sight.

Glossary of terms used in this book

Argentine Tango - AR-jen-teen TANG/oh, *the reason you bought this book*

Biagi - Be-Adg-ee – *a pianist who specialized in syncopated tango music and formed his own orchestra.*

Boleo – boh-LAY-oh, *an arcing movement of the foot.*

Buenos Aires - BWEN-oss EYE-reez, *capital of Argentina and the spiritual home of Argentine Tango, often abbreviated to BsAs.*

Cabeceo - cah-beh-SAY-oh, *non-verbal method of asking for dances, see Chapter 5 for more information.*

Códigos – CO-dee-gohs, *a code of conduct for the milonga, which varies from venue to venue.*

Corrida - corr-REE-dah [but trilled], *a short series of tiny 'running' steps.*

Cortina – cor-TEEN-ah, *the cortina is a short piece of music played between each tanda. A tanda is a usually a set of three or four pieces of music intended for dancing tango. Ideally the cortina is sufficiently different from the music being played for dancing. The floor is usually cleared, except for people wishing to continue dancing together. They can choose to either remain where they are, or stay together and move off to the side, so as not to obstruct others from cabeceoing each other.*

Di Sarli - Dee SAR-lee, *a famous Argentine tango composer, pianist and orchestra leader.*

Embrace - *the way the partners hold each other in the dance*

La Cumparsita - la kuum-par-SEE-tah, *traditionally the last song played to signal the end of the milonga.*

La Planchadora - la plan-cha-DOR-ah, *a woman who sits all night at the milonga without being asked to dance.*

Mirada – mee-RA-da, *looking at someone to invite them to dance.*

Milonga - mee-LON-ga, *the place where tango dancers go to dance socially, as well as a rhythmic style of tango music.*

Nuevo – nu-AY-vo, *a style of dancing, a teaching methodology and a genre of tango music.*

Podestá – po-deh-STAH, *a famous tango singer.*

Prácticas – PRAC-tee-cas, *practice sessions.*

Ronda – RON-dah, *the flow of dancers cooperating and dancing together in harmony as they gradually move anti-clockwise around the room, generally without changing lanes.*

Valses – VAL-ses, *a vals, singular, is one of the styles of music that tango is danced to. For more information on Birthday valses, see Chapter 10.*

Villa Urquiza - VEE-zha ur-QUEE-sah, *a specific style of tango dancing, as well as an area in Buenos Aires.*

Volcada – vol/CAH/da - *the follower is titled forward off their axis.*

BONUS

The current conventional wisdom, is that I should now ask you to leave a review about this book and then, in return, offer you a bonus after you've done that. However, because this will make a big difference to both your enjoyment of tango, and indeed life, I'm giving the bonus to you now. Of course if you'd like to leave me a review, that'd be great too.

Expect the best outcome. Afterwards, ask "What could have gone better?"

Whatever you do, don't think of Pink Elephants dancing in tutus! You just did, didn't you? Our brains process negatives by "looking up" what they're being told "not to do". So telling someone "don't fall", will make them think of falling, which is usually unhelpful. Whereas "hang on", or "relax" bring to mind more useful information.

The same applies to tango and well, a lot of things in life. If you enter a milonga asking yourself what could go wrong, that's the information your brain will be processing. And it'll be processing away in your subconscious for the rest of the evening, coloring how you see the world. But if you ask yourself what could go right, your brain will help you out that way.

Ok, but this is just a Woo, Hippie, Pollyanna thing, right? You feel happier, but that's it? Strangely, no. There are tangible benefits too.

Scientists conducted an experiment where they asked people who considered themselves either very lucky or very unlucky, to apply. They were given directions to the laboratory, and on the way there, the scientists placed a winning lottery ticket on the pavement. All the people who considered themselves unlucky walked straight past it. After all, if it was on the ground, surely it was worthless.

However, the "lucky" people stopped to check and got a winning lottery ticket, because they chose to take a few seconds to lean down and check. There's a lot of opportunities in social tango that you'll either take, or let pass you by, depending on whether you go in thinking things are going to be awful, or great.

Similarly, after the milonga, don't beat yourself up over the things that didn't turn out so great, as this tends to take you farther away from finding new, more helpful answers. Mulling on how awful something was is also a really unpleasant experience to repeatedly put yourself through. Instead, ask yourself what could have been better and how could it have gone better? Your brain will then try to find those helpful answers.

- - -

Ok, that's really it. Thanks for reading my book and I hope it brings you a better tango experience.

Oliver Kent